THE
BOOKS OF THE BIBLE
STUDY JOURNAL

THE
BOOKS OF THE BIBLE
STUDY JOURNAL

ZONDERVAN®

ZONDERVAN

Books of the Bible Study Journal
Copyright © 2017 by Zondervan

This title is also available as a Zondervan ebook.

Requests for information should be addressed to:
Zondervan, 3900 Sparks Dr. SE, Grand Rapids, Michigan 49546

ISBN 978-0-310-08605-5

Cover illustrations: Shutterstock
Interior design: Denise Froehlich

First Printing October 2017 / Printed in the United States of America

Contents

The Community Bible Experience 7

COVENANT HISTORY

INTRODUCTORY SESSION 17
WEEK 1: Genesis 21
WEEK 2: Exodus 26
WEEK 3: Leviticus, Numbers 33
WEEK 4: Numbers, Deuteronomy 40
WEEK 5: Joshua, Judges 47
WEEK 6: Ruth, Samuel–Kings 54
WEEK 7: Samuel–Kings 61
WEEK 8: Samuel–Kings 66

THE PROPHETS

INTRODUCTORY SESSION 75
WEEK 1: Jonah, Amos, Hosea, Micah, Isaiah 81
WEEK 2: Isaiah 88
WEEK 3: Isaiah, Zephaniah, Nahum, Habakkuk 95
WEEK 4: Jeremiah 101
WEEK 5: Jeremiah 106
WEEK 6: Obadiah, Ezekiel 111
WEEK 7: Ezekiel 117
WEEK 8: Haggai, Zechariah, Joel, Malachi 124

THE WRITINGS

INTRODUCTORY SESSION...........................133

WEEK 1: Psalms 138

WEEK 2: Psalms.. 144

WEEK 3: Psalms, Lamentations, Song of Songs........... 150

WEEK 4: Proverbs, Ecclesiastes 156

WEEK 5: Job...162

WEEK 6: Chronicles-Ezra-Nehemiah 168

WEEK 7: Chronicles-Ezra-Nehemiah 175

WEEK 8: Esther, Daniel 182

THE NEW TESTAMENT

INTRODUCTORY SESSION...........................191

WEEK 1: Luke–Acts.....................................195

WEEK 2: Luke–Acts, 1–2 Thessalonians 201

WEEK 3: 1–2 Corinthians, Galatians, Romans 209

WEEK 4: Romans, Colossians, Ephesians, Philemon,
Philippians, 1 Timothy, Titus, 2 Timothy...............218

WEEK 5: Matthew 225

WEEK 6: Hebrews, James, Mark 232

WEEK 7: 1–2 Peter, Jude, John 239

WEEK 8: 1–3 John, Revelation 246

The Community Bible Experience

A Better Bible Experience

What would happen if we actually read the Bible? Not a verse here or there, but the whole Bible?

What if, instead of going it alone, we could have a real conversation about the Bible—one anyone can join, no matter where they are in their faith journey?

The Community Bible Experience is about reading the Bible as it was meant to be read—whole books, in community. It will take you beyond Bible study, beyond reading in fragments, and beyond reading in isolation.

Discover the complete story. Let's read big, read real, and read together.

How It Works

1. **Read big.** You'll cover the whole Bible in a series of four 8-week segments—reading 5 days a week, around 12 pages a day. The average day's reading takes 30 minutes or so to complete.
2. **Read real.** You'll use a groundbreaking presentation of the Scriptures, called *The Books of the Bible*. It's designed to feel more like reading the original.
3. **Read together.** You'll meet with your discussion group once a week for book club-style conversations about the Bible.

A Unique Bible

During the Community Bible Experience, you'll read from a revolutionary presentation of Scripture called *The Books of the Bible.*

When you open your copy, the first thing you'll notice is that this is no ordinary Bible. There are no chapter or verse numbers. No study notes or cross references. No red lettering.

That's because none of these features are original to the Scriptures. Most were added centuries later to help us find things. But the Bible isn't a reference book; first and foremost, it's a story. It's a collection of books, each of which was meant to be experienced as a whole. Modern Bible formatting imposes a different structure on the text, one that encourages us to read in fragments.

The Books of the Bible is designed to be read from beginning to end. We've stripped away centuries of artificial formatting, leaving behind nothing but pure Bible text in a presentation that's easier to read and understand.

We've formatted each book so you can see the natural section breaks put there by the authors. We've rearranged the books for easier understanding—for example, putting Paul's letters in a more chronological order (instead of longest to shortest), so you can follow along more easily.

The Books of the Bible features the complete text of the Bible in four volumes using the New International Version®, the most widely read contemporary English translation of the Bible.

DURING YOUR JOURNEY

Five Tips for Reading

1. **Read what you can.**

   Don't get discouraged if you fall behind. Keep at it, even if you don't make it all the way through each day's reading. If you have trouble keeping up, listening to the audio version can help.

2. **Read every day.**

    Plan on reading five days a week, Monday through Friday. The pace is a little intense, but reading large portions of Scripture is also incredibly rewarding.

3. **Be fully present.**

    Avoid distraction while reading. (Turns out we're not that good at multitasking.) Instead, devote your full attention to the text.

4. **Read the book intros.**

    The Books of the Bible includes brief introductions or "invitations" to each book, unpacking the context and literary structure of what you're about to read. Trust us, they're well worth your time.

5. **Don't worry about the parts you don't understand.**

    The goal is to read big, not to catch every detail. You can always go back and study a specific passage in greater detail later. For now, take in the big picture; let that be your focus as you read.

Reading Plan

Read five days a week, Monday through Friday. Most readings take around 30 minutes to complete. Some daily readings are longer or shorter, because each one ends at the close of a book or a natural section break within a book. Section breaks are indicated by line spaces—the bigger the space, the bigger the break.

Reading Sequence

The Books of the Bible is divided into four volumes: Covenant History, The Prophets, The Writings, and The New Testament. These volumes can be read in different sequences, depending on the preferences and needs of your group.

- **Traditional sequence:** Covenant History, The Prophets, The Writings, The New Testament
- **New Testament first:** The New Testament, Covenant History, The Prophets, The Writings

- **New Testament twice:** The New Testament, Covenant History, The Prophets, The Writings, The New Testament
- **New Testament only:** The New Testament

Reading Schedule

Like the reading sequence, the reading schedule may be adapted to accommodate the desires and needs of your group. There are a total of 32 weeks of readings, 8 weeks per volume, and a variety of ways to schedule them:

- **Whole Bible in one year:** Early Fall, Late Fall, Winter, Spring
- **One volume per year:** January Year 1, January Year 2, January Year 3, January Year 4
- **One volume per semester:** Winter Year 1, Fall Year 1, Winter Year 2, Fall Year 2

SHARING THE JOURNEY

Planning Your Weekly Gatherings

Discussion groups should meet once a week during the Community Bible Experience.

When should we meet?

> If possible, meet on weekends. There are no readings assigned for Saturday and Sunday, which makes the weekend a good time to get together.

How often should we meet?

> Each volume of *The Books of the Bible* is broken into eight weeks of readings, but **plan on meeting nine times for each volume.** Have an introductory gathering the week before you start reading, then meet once a week for the next eight weeks to discuss the readings for that volume. If you are reading straight through all four volumes, you only need to have one introductory gathering which would take place before you begin your first volume.

How much time should we spend together?

Most discussion groups meet for 60–90 minutes each week, but feel free to adjust this based on the needs of your group.

What Will We Cover?

Each week, you will spend the first 30–60 minutes sharing your reflections on the text with your discussion group, using these five simple conversation starters:

1. What was new or compelling to you?
2. What questions did you have?
3. Was there anything that bothered you?
4. What did you learn about loving God?
5. What did you learn about loving others?

During the last 15–30 minutes of your meeting, you will be preparing for the week ahead by watching a video of a Bible teacher explaining the significance of the Scriptures you are about to read.

Three Tips for Weekly Gatherings

If you've been part of a Bible study before, you might find these gatherings a bit different. Here are three tips to help you get the most from them.

1. **Think "book club."**

    Treat your weekly gatherings more like a book club than a traditional Bible study. The discussions are meant to be free-flowing and wide-ranging.

    You may come to each week's gathering with lots of specific questions. That's okay. It's what happens when you read 12 pages a day! Try to focus your conversation on the big picture—where the overall story is moving as is the part we're invited to play in it. To help, you can suggest your group keeps a "parking lot" list of questions to explore further after your journey.

2. **Honor each participant, wherever they are in their journey.**

It's likely your fellow readers come from a variety of backgrounds. You may hold different perspectives or assumptions about the Bible. Some of you may be lifelong students of the text; others may be brand new to it. Remember, each person has something meaningful to add to the conversation.

3. **Listen actively, speak freely.**

Welcome every voice in the conversation, and don't hesitate to add your own. You never know how someone else might benefit by hearing what was new or compelling to you, what questions you had, or what you wrestled with.

How God took up residence

IN THE GOOD CREATION

AS HIS COSMIC TEMPLE,

the attempt by humans to

REBEL AGAINST GOD'S

GRACIOUS RULE AND SEIZE

CONTROL OF THE WORLD,

and the unveiling of

THE CREATOR'S PLAN

TO CHOOSE ISRAEL AS HIS MEANS

OF BRINGING LIGHT AND LIFE

back to all peoples.

COVENANT HISTORY

INVITATION TO
COVENANT HISTORY

One continuous story runs through the first quarter of the Bible, covering all the books from Genesis to Samuel–Kings. It's the story of the nation of Israel, told through a progression of covenants God made with the ancestors and people of Israel over the course of their history, thus the name of this volume, Covenant History.

To rescue humanity from rebellion and misery, God made his first covenant with one man, Abraham, promising that through him and his descendants everyone in the world would be blessed. When those descendants had grown into the nation of Israel, God brought them out of Egypt and made a further covenant with them; they were to follow God's laws in order to provide a living demonstration of God's goodness and wisdom to all the nations around them. Later, God made a covenant with one of their kings, David, promising that one of his descendants would always be on the throne of Israel.

Unfortunately, the people didn't honor their agreements with God. Consequently, their nation was ultimately destroyed and they were scattered. At this point, the narrative of the Covenant History stops. But it's clear that the story itself hasn't come to an end. The covenant promises God made can't be undone, even by human unfaithfulness. God will continue to act on behalf of this nation and work through it to reach all nations. How God does this is related in the books that make up the rest of the Bible.

INTRODUCTORY SESSION

The Introductory Session introduces your group to *The Books of the Bible, Covenant History.* Hold the Introductory Session the week before your first meeting. If you are reading straight through all four volumes, you will only hold one Introductory Session, which will take place before you begin your first volume. If you are spreading out your reading of the four volumes, it is helpful to have an introductory gathering the week before you start each one.

Getting to Know You (15–30 minutes)

If your group is new to each other, or if you have any new members in your group for this session, invite each group member to introduce themselves, using any or all of the following prompts:

- List three of your roles in life and what you like about them.
- What one word describes your past experience of reading the Bible?
- What do you hope to get from this journey of reading *The Books of the Bible, Covenant History* together?

Introduction (15–30 minutes)

INTRODUCE THE
COMMUNITY BIBLE EXPERIENCE

Explain how the Community Bible Experience works by summarizing the information in the book introduction, starting on page 7 of this study journal. The key points are:

- Five tips for Bible reading
- Weekly reading plan
- Weekly discussion questions for groups
- Three tips for weekly gatherings

Allow time for discussion about how your group wants to function with each other and to address any concerns people have about doing the Bible reading.

INTRODUCE *COVENANT HISTORY*

The Books of the Bible, Covenant History contains six sections of important introductory material. If time allows, read through all six sections of the introductory material together. If your group has read other volumes in the past, or if you have time constraints, focus on the Drama of the Bible in Six Acts, page iii (it's helpful to read that together before every new series), and read the Invitation to the Covenant History, page xiv.

Preparing for the Week Ahead (15–20 minutes)

Discuss the challenge of reading 12 pages a day. Remind participants that most readings take around 30 minutes to complete—about the same time it takes to watch a short TV show.

WATCH VIDEO WEEK 1: GENESIS

To get the most out of what you will be reading in the coming week, close your time together by watching the video of Bible teacher John Walton explaining the themes and relevance of Genesis. Use the following outline to jot down any additional insights or questions.

VIDEO NOTES

The Old Testament gives us God's story, God's revelation of his plans and purposes.

The Old Testament has authority: We have a responsibility to submit to it.

We have to read it in context: literary context and cultural context.

Purpose of Genesis

Introduces the presence of God

The story of the Bible: God's plan is to reestablish his presence.

Covenant: the mechanism of establishing the presence of God

Overview of Genesis

Genesis 1–11: How God's presence was lost and how people tried to regain it

Genesis 12–50: God's counterinitiative in the covenant with Abraham

Themes of Genesis

Creation: God brings order. Why?

God orders creation to be a sacred space, so he can dwell among his people.

Disorder: By eating of the tree of knowledge of good and evil, we want to make ourselves like God.

God reestablishes order through the covenant.

The Israelites were God's instrument to reveal himself.

Importance of Genesis

The patriarchs are not heroes, but rather show God's plans and purposes.

"You intended to harm me, but God intended it for good to accomplish what is now being done, the saving of many lives."

(GENESIS 50:20)

THIS WEEK

Read the book of Genesis in *The Books of the Bible, Covenant History.* Maintain your momentum by keeping these guidelines in mind:

- Read what you can.
- Read something every day.
- Always have your *Books of the Bible* with you.
- Every week is a new week.
- Use this study journal as you do your reading for Week 1: Genesis, recording any thoughts on the Daily Reading Journal page.

WEEK 1

GENESIS

GENESIS

The book of Genesis is the first of five chronicles that make up Covenant History. A chronicle is a literary method of conveying historical material as a series of stories based on a list of people or places. In Genesis, the chronicle is based on a list of people. The stories about the 11 people on the list are introduced by the phrase *this is the account of [person X]*. The general pattern is that after briefly considering their siblings, Genesis focuses on the individuals in each generation that God is working through to fulfill his promises.

What to watch for in Genesis: This book is an ancient record of the origins of humanity and the beginnings of God's plan to restore order in the world he created. Look for all the instances where Genesis explains how something came to be.

 PERSONAL BIBLE EXPERIENCE

Your personal Bible experience starts with a daily practice of reading the Bible. This week before your group meeting, read the book of Genesis. Use the journaling space to capture your thoughts, questions, responses, emotions, and insights as you read the daily selection. Keep in mind the questions you will be talking about with your discussion group:

- What was new or compelling to you?
- What questions did you have?
- Was there anything that bothered you?
- What did you learn about loving God?
- What did you learn about loving others?

Daily Reading Journal

Day 1: Genesis Invitation–11:26 (pages 1–17)

_____

_____

_____

_____

_____

Day 2: Genesis 11:27–25:18 (pages 18–37)

_____

_____

_____

_____

_____

Day 3: Genesis 25:19–35:29 (pages 38–56)

_____

_____

_____

_____

_____

Day 4: Genesis 36:1–41:57 (pages 57–67)

_____

_____

_____

_____

_____

Day 5: Genesis 42:1–50:26 (pages 67–83)

_____

_____

_____

_____

_____

COMMUNITY BIBLE EXPERIENCE

Welcome to Session 1 of the Community Bible Experience. You have been experiencing the Bible personally by reading through the book of Genesis this week, and now your group has gathered to experience the Bible in community with one another. Think of your discussion as more of a book club than a Bible study.

Reflecting on the Previous Week (30–60 minutes)

From your Personal Bible Experience in Genesis this week, have a conversation with your group about what you read by answering the following questions.

What was new or compelling to you?

What questions did you have?

Was there anything that bothered you?

What did you learn about loving God?

What did you learn about loving others?

Preparing for the Week Ahead (15–20 minutes)

WATCH VIDEO WEEK 2: EXODUS

To get the most out of what you will be reading in the coming week, close your time together by watching the video of Bible teacher John Walton explaining the themes and relevance of Exodus. Use the following outline to jot down any additional insights or questions.

VIDEO NOTES

Where are the promises of God?

Where is God?

Purpose of Exodus

Moses signals the beginning of God's presence among his people again.

Focus of Exodus

The reestablishment of God's presence in the tabernacle

Through Israel, all the world is blessed through God's presence.

Plagues deliver God's people and demonstrate his character.

Israel is a kingdom of priests (Exodus 19:4–6).

Torah is given so that God's people can dwell within his presence.

Law is not legislation but wisdom for holiness.

Torah is connected to the tabernacle.

Relevance of Exodus

Unfolds God's plans and purposes to dwell among his people

Learn God's inclination and capabilities.

Wisdom to live in the presence of God

What is God doing, and how can I be a part of it?

THIS WEEK

Read the book of Exodus in *The Books of the Bible, Covenant History.*
Maintain your momentum by keeping these guidelines in mind:

- Read what you can.
- Read something every day.
- Always have your *Books of the Bible* with you.
- Every week is a new week.
- Use this study journal as you do your reading for Week 2: Exodus, recording any thoughts on the Daily Reading Journal page.

WEEK 2
EXODUS

EXODUS
· · · · · · · ·

In the book of Exodus, the second chronicle in the Covenant History begins, and this one continues through the books of Leviticus and Numbers too. This chronicle is based not on a list of people, as we saw in Genesis, but on a list of places, or travel notices, such as, *The Israelites journeyed from Ramses to Sukkoth.* What happened at each place they stopped is described after each notice. One location, Mount Sinai, is given far more attention than the others; the second half of Exodus, all of Leviticus, and the beginning of Numbers take place there.

What to watch for in Exodus: This book is rich with foreshadowing of Jesus our Savior. Look for clues about the Messiah in the person of Moses, in the Passover, the meaning of the seven feasts, the Exodus, the provision of manna and water, the tabernacle, and the institution of high priest.

 PERSONAL BIBLE EXPERIENCE
· ·

Your personal Bible experience starts with a daily practice of reading the Bible. This week before your group meeting, read the book of Exodus. Use the journaling space to capture your thoughts, questions, responses, emotions, and insights as you read the daily selection. Keep in mind the questions you will be talking about with your discussion group:

- What was new or compelling to you?
- What questions did you have?
- Was there anything that bothered you?
- What did you learn about loving God?
- What did you learn about loving others?

Daily Reading Journal

Day 6: Exodus Invitation–12:28 (pages 85–105)

_____

_____

_____

_____

_____

Day 7: Exodus 12:29–18:27 (pages 105–116)

_____

_____

_____

_____

_____

Day 8: Exodus 19:1–24:18 (pages 116–124)

_____

_____

_____

_____

_____

Day 9: Exodus 25:1–34:35 (pages 124–139)

_____

_____

_____

_____

_____

Day 10: Exodus 35:1–40:38 (pages 139–148)

_____

_____

_____

_____

_____

COMMUNITY BIBLE EXPERIENCE

Welcome to Session 2 of the Community Bible Experience. You have been experiencing the Bible personally by reading through the book of Exodus this week, and now your group has gathered to experience the Bible in community with each other. Think of your discussion as more of a book club than a Bible study.

Reflecting on the Previous Week (30–60 minutes)

From your Personal Bible Experience in Exodus this week, have a conversation with your group about what you read by answering the following questions.

What was new or compelling to you?

What questions did you have?

Was there anything that bothered you?

What did you learn about loving God?

What did you learn about loving others?

Preparing for the Week Ahead (15–20 minutes)

WATCH VIDEO WEEK 3: LEVITICUS, NUMBERS 1–19

To get the most out of what you will be reading in the coming week, close your time together by watching the video of Bible teacher John Walton explaining the themes and relevance of Leviticus and Numbers 1–19. Use the following outline to jot down any additional insights or questions.

VIDEO NOTES

Leviticus continues the story of God's presence: How can we host the presence of God?

Purpose of Leviticus

Written to detail how to care for sacred space

Understanding Holiness

Holiness is intrinsic to Immanuel theology.

Holiness is a status granted by God.

Holiness co-identifies us with God.

Holiness is not something we can gain or lose.

Holiness is a status connected to divine presence.

Purpose of Rituals

Sacrifices are "relationship-building" activities.

Sin and guilt offerings cleanse sacred space.

Day of Atonement (Leviticus 16)

Rituals are not about salvation.

Purpose of Priests

Priests are guardians of sacred space.

Priests mediate revelation.

Priests mediate access.

Priests mediate worship.

There's a difference between the temple and church.

Relevance of Leviticus

Instruction on how to live in the presence of God

It's not about what we do, but about understanding holiness.

Living into the identity of holiness God has given us

Numbers 1–19

Themes of Numbers

Traveling with God

Testing God

Spies

Failure to enter land

Relevance of Numbers

God's faithfulness despite Israel's unfaithfulness

THIS WEEK
· · · · · · · · · ·

Read the books of Leviticus and the first half of Numbers in *The Books of the Bible, Covenant History*. Maintain your momentum by keeping these guidelines in mind:

- Read what you can.
- Read something every day.
- Always have your *Books of the Bible* with you.
- Every week is a new week.
- Use this study journal as you do your reading for Week 3: Leviticus, Numbers, recording any thoughts on the Daily Reading Journal pages.

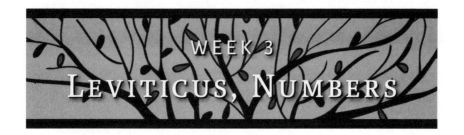

LEVITICUS

We are still camped at Mount Sinai in the book of Leviticus, where more of God's commands for the Israelites are given. There are four types of laws that are to govern Israel's conduct: laws about offerings, cleanness, holiness, and redemption. There is a dynamic relationship between these. The basic state of any created thing is that it is *clean* and common. When certain things are set apart for God's purposes, they become *holy*. But that can't happen if they've become unclean. *Offerings* are the means of moving something from unclean back to clean, or from common to holy. *Redemption* is a special process that restores people to places and relationships from which they've become alienated.

What to watch for in Leviticus: As with Exodus, look for allusions to the person and work of Jesus Christ in the offerings, feasts, and role of the high priest, and look forward with thankfulness to the time we will read about in the New Testament when Jesus will satisfy all these requirements once and for all.

NUMBERS

The book of Numbers brings the Israelites the rest of the way from Egypt to the borders of the land of Canaan. But it's not a straightforward journey. Numbers is a book of wanderings. It records the failure of Israel to believe in the promise of God and the resulting judgment of wandering in the wilderness for forty years.

What to watch for in Numbers: In this book of divine discipline, see how God takes Israel from a nation in its infancy through the painful process of testing and maturation that comes by experiencing the consequences of irresponsible decisions.

PERSONAL BIBLE EXPERIENCE

Your personal Bible experience starts with a daily practice of reading the Bible. This week before your group meeting, read the books of Leviticus and the first half of Numbers. Use the journaling space to capture your thoughts, questions, responses, emotions, and insights as you read the daily selection. Keep in mind the questions you will be talking about with your discussion group:

- What was new or compelling to you?
- What questions did you have?
- Was there anything that bothered you?
- What did you learn about loving God?
- What did you learn about loving others?

Daily Reading Journal

Day 11: Leviticus 1:1–10:20 (pages 149–162)

_____

_____

_____

_____

_____

_____

Day 12: Leviticus 11:1–16:34 (pages 162–174)

_____

_____

_____

_____

_____

_____

Day 13: Leviticus 17:1–27:34 (pages 174–192)

_____
_____
_____
_____
_____
_____

Day 14: Numbers 1:1–10:10 (pages 193–212)

_____
_____
_____
_____
_____
_____

Day 15: Numbers 10:11–19:22 (pages 212–227)

_____
_____
_____
_____
_____
_____

 **COMMUNITY BIBLE EXPERIENCE**

Welcome to Session 3 of the Community Bible Experience. You have been experiencing the Bible personally by reading through the books of Leviticus and the first half of Numbers this week, and now your group has gathered to experience the Bible in community with each other. Think of your discussion as more of a book club than a Bible study.

Reflecting on the Previous Week (30–60 minutes)

From your Personal Bible Experience in Leviticus and Numbers this week, have a conversation with your group about what you read by answering the following questions.

What was new or compelling to you?

What questions did you have?

Was there anything that bothered you?

What did you learn about loving God?

What did you learn about loving others?

Preparing for the Week Ahead (15–20 minutes)

WATCH VIDEO WEEK 4: NUMBERS 20–36, DEUTERONOMY

To get the most out of what you will be reading in the coming week, close your time together by watching the video of Bible teacher John Walton explaining the themes and relevance of Numbers 20–36 and Deuteronomy. Use the following outline to jot down any additional insights or questions.

VIDEO NOTES

Numbers 20–36

Numbers transitions from the first to the second generation.

Moses's crime: "Because you did not trust in me enough to honor me as holy in the sight of the Israelites, you will not bring this community into the land I give them." (Numbers 20:12)

Balaam: God's means of giving promises to the next generation

Structure of Deuteronomy

Vassal treaty and land grants

Three addresses by Moses

Purpose of Deuteronomy

To formalize the covenant from Sinai

To convey the importance of God's "Name"

To show the Law as an act of grace: "See, I set before you today life and prosperity, death and destruction. . . . Now choose life" (Deuteronomy 30:15, 19).

The Ten Commandments (Exodus 20; Deuteronomy 5)

Saying 1: No Other Gods

Saying 2: No Idols

Images were ways the gods mediated their presence.

God says: no artificial mediation.

Saying 3: Taking the Lord's Name in Vain

Acting as if the name of the Lord is powerless

The saying is against using the name of the Lord for their own purposes.

There is power in the name of God because it represents God.

Identity theft assumes power.

Saying 4: Sabbath

Sabbath is connected to God's rest among his people.

God ordered the world in order to rule it.

Sabbath is participating with God as we pursue God's order.

Themes of Deuteronomy

Covenant and Torah

Central sanctuary

History as theology

God's people as his partners

THIS WEEK

Read the rest of Numbers and the book of Deuteronomy in *The Books of the Bible, Covenant History*. Maintain your momentum by keeping these guidelines in mind:

- Read what you can.
- Read something every day.
- Always have your *Books of the Bible* with you.
- Every week is a new week.
- Use this study journal as you do your reading for Week 4: Numbers, Deuteronomy, recording any thoughts on the Daily Reading Journal pages.

DEUTERONOMY

At the end of the forty years of wandering through the wilderness, Moses gives a long farewell address to the Israelites. This speech renews the covenant with God, taking the same form and pattern of the treaties that kings of the time would make with other kings who were subject to them. This particular literary form structures the book of Deuteronomy, making it an exception among the chronicles that generally make up the Covenant History.

What to watch for in Deuteronomy: Rather than seeing Deuteronomy as a repetition of previous books, look for the five elements of a kingly treaty:

1. List of the name and titles of the ruler
2. Recounting of the mighty acts of the ruler
3. Obligations of the servant
4. Blessings for keeping the treaty and cursings for breaking it
5. Witnesses to the treaty and provisions for maintaining it

 PERSONAL BIBLE EXPERIENCE

Your personal Bible experience starts with a daily practice of reading the Bible. This week before your group meeting, read the rest of Numbers and the book of Deuteronomy. Use the journaling space to capture your thoughts, questions, responses, emotions, and insights as you read the daily selection. Keep in mind the questions you will be talking about with your discussion group:

- What was new or compelling to you?
- What questions did you have?
- Was there anything that bothered you?
- What did you learn about loving God?
- What did you learn about loving others?

Daily Reading Journal

Day 16: Numbers 20:1–27:11 (pages 227–242)

_____

_____

_____

_____

_____

Day 17: Numbers 27:12–36:13 (pages 242–256)

_____

_____

_____

_____

_____

Day 18: Deuteronomy Invitation–11:32 (pages 257–277)

_____

_____

_____

_____

_____

Day 19: Deuteronomy 12:1–26:19 (pages 277–294)

_____

_____

_____

_____

Day 20: Deuteronomy 27:1–34:12 (pages 294–311)

 **COMMUNITY BIBLE EXPERIENCE**

Welcome to Session 4 of the Community Bible Experience. You have been experiencing the Bible personally by reading through the rest of Numbers and the book of Deuteronomy this week, and now your group has gathered to experience the Bible in community with each other. Think of your discussion as more of a book club than a Bible study.

Reflecting on the Previous Week (30–60 minutes)

From your Personal Bible Experience in Numbers and Deuteronomy this week, have a conversation with your group about what you read by answering the following questions.

What was new or compelling to you?

What questions did you have?

Was there anything that bothered you?

What did you learn about loving God?

What did you learn about loving others?

Preparing for the Week Ahead (15–20 minutes)

WATCH VIDEO WEEK 5: JOSHUA, JUDGES

To get the most out of what you will be reading in the coming week, close your time together by watching the video of Bible teacher John Walton explaining the themes and relevance of Joshua and Judges. Use the following outline to jot down any additional insights or questions.

VIDEO NOTES

How to Read Narrative

The importance of story: it has a beginning, middle, and end.

Understand these books as literature before we understand them as history.

We can only know people as characters.

The goal is to understand the narrator, not to reconstruct events.

The event is not inspired; the interpretation of the event is inspired.

Selective; to emphasize certain truths

Purpose of Joshua

God providing the land he promised

Rahab (Joshua 2): "We know God has given you the land."

Structure of Joshua

Preparing to enter the land

Conquests

Land distribution

Covenant renewal

Themes of Joshua

Covenant and land

The "ban": that which does not belong has to be removed so that God can dwell on earth

Divine Warrior

Judges

Israel has trouble gaining control of the land and being the people of God.

Covers four hundred-plus years

Purpose of Judges

Shows people's failure and unfaithfulness

God's faithfulness through judges (deliverers)

Themes of Judges

Cycles: unfaithfulness, troubles, crying out, God's deliverer

Judges: Military deliverers bringing justice from oppressors

Spirit of the Lord: God's power and authority working through them

Relevance of Joshua and Judges

They show us how God carries out his plans and purposes with his people.

We see what kind of God he is so we can partner with him as we know him.

THIS WEEK

Read the books of Joshua and Judges in *The Books of the Bible, Covenant History*. Maintain your momentum by keeping these guidelines in mind:

- Read what you can.
- Read something every day.
- Always have your *Books of the Bible* with you.
- Every week is a new week.
- Use this study journal as you do your reading for Week 5: Joshua, Judges, recording any thoughts on the Daily Reading Journal pages.

WEEK 5
JOSHUA, JUDGES

JOSHUA

The book of Joshua resumes the "chronicle" pattern we have seen in the Covenant History. This chronicle is built out of a list of kings the Israelites defeat when they invade Canaan. The rest of the book looks at how the land was divided among the tribes. As at the first creation, God is making an appropriate home for his people. But the book also specifies that pockets of resistance remained. In keeping with the general theme of the Covenant History, Joshua leads the people in renewing the covenant they made with God before they entered the land.

What to watch for in Joshua: The leader, Joshua, who was born a slave in Egypt, is worth our attention. Look for his qualities of obedient faith, courage, and dedication to God and his Word.

JUDGES

The chronicle of this book is based on the list of twelve judges of Israel. Because Israel had limited success in driving out the remaining Canaanites, they tried to live with them instead, with disastrous results. The judges were the leaders God raised up to deliver them from conquering nations whenever they cried out for help, but soon they would lapse into unfaithfulness again. The phrase *again the Israelites did evil in the eyes of the* LORD introduces each successive judge in the lineup, but the repeated deterioration takes its toll, leaving Israel primed for a king.

What to watch for in Judges: Identify the cycle that repeats itself several times in Judges: Israel turns away from God; they are oppressed by their enemies; they cry out to God for help; they are delivered by their leaders.

PERSONAL BIBLE EXPERIENCE

Your personal Bible experience starts with a daily practice of reading the Bible. This week before your group meeting, read the books of Joshua and Judges. Use the journaling space to capture your thoughts, questions, responses, emotions, and insights as you read the daily selection. Keep in mind the questions you will be talking about with your discussion group:

- What was new or compelling to you?
- What questions did you have?
- Was there anything that bothered you?
- What did you learn about loving God?
- What did you learn about loving others?

Daily Reading Journal

Day 21: Joshua–Judges Invitation–Joshua 12:24 (pages 313–333)

_____

_____

_____

_____

_____

_____

Day 22: Joshua 13:1–24:33 (pages 333–351)

_____

_____

_____

_____

_____

_____

Day 23: Judges 1:1–8:32 (pages 353–367)

_____

_____

_____

_____

_____

_____

Day 24: Judges 8:33–16:31 (pages 367–381)

_____

_____

_____

_____

_____

Day 25: Judges 17:1–21:25 (pages 381–388)

_____

_____

_____

_____

_____

_____

COMMUNITY BIBLE EXPERIENCE

Welcome to Session 5 of the Community Bible Experience. You have been experiencing the Bible personally by reading through the books of Joshua and Judges this week, and now your group has gathered to experience the Bible in community with each other. Think of your discussion as more of a book club than a Bible study.

Reflecting on the Previous Week (30–60 minutes)

From your Personal Bible Experience in Joshua and Judges this week, have a conversation with your group about what you read by answering the following questions.

What was new or compelling to you?

What questions did you have?

Was there anything that bothered you?

What did you learn about loving God?

What did you learn about loving others?

Preparing for the Week Ahead (15–20 minutes)

WATCH VIDEO WEEK 6: RUTH, SAMUEL–KINGS

To get the most out of what you will be reading in the coming week, close your time together by watching the video of Bible teacher John Walton explaining the themes and relevance of Ruth and Samuel–Kings. Use the following outline to jot down any additional insights or questions.

VIDEO NOTES

Purpose of Ruth

In contrast to the time of Judges, faithfulness survived in individuals.

Faith like David's makes more sense in the monarchy if people like Ruth and Boaz existed during the period of the judges.

Ruth is similar to God's preservation in Egypt: "Don't urge me to leave you or to turn back from you. Where you go I will go, and where you stay I will stay. Your people will be my people and your God my God" (Ruth 1:16).

Themes of Ruth

Hesed: acting to fulfill an obligation

Understand what it is that impresses God: faithfulness.

1 Samuel–2 Samuel 5:3

Purpose of Samuel

Establishment of the Davidic Covenant

Overview of Samuel

Role of Samuel

Ark narratives

Requesting a king: The king is in the driver's seat instead of God; this is what is unacceptable.

Saul's kingship

Man after God's own heart: God following his own heart, not David following his heart

David and Goliath

David, Jonathan, and Saul

Themes of Samuel

God is king of his people.

God chooses.

Relevance of Ruth and Samuel

Seeing God at work to reveal his design for kingship shows us who God chooses as instruments to carry out his plans and purposes.

We don't try to be like Ruth or David but the kind of people God needs in our place to be his instruments.

THIS WEEK
· · · · · · · · · ·

Read the books of Ruth and the first part of Samuel–Kings in *The Books of the Bible, Covenant History*. Maintain your momentum by keeping these guidelines in mind:

- Read what you can.
- Read something every day.
- Always have your *Books of the Bible* with you.
- Every week is a new week.
- Use this study journal as you do your reading for Week 6: Ruth, Samuel–Kings, recording any thoughts on the Daily Reading Journal pages.

RUTH, SAMUEL–KINGS

RUTH
· · · · ·

The book of Ruth contributes to Israel's transition to the monarchy. It represents another distinct literary form, a conversational drama, where a series of scenes feature a short narrative introduction, then a dialogue between the characters. The story of Ruth is a message to Israel, defending David's right to be king even though he is descended from a Moabite woman. God's original covenant with Abraham promised that *all peoples on earth* would be blessed through his descendants, so God's higher goals will find their expression in David's kingship.

What to watch for in Ruth: Consider as you read the book of Ruth how we can each play our own part in God's purposes by being people of kindness, goodwill, and generosity to outsiders.

SAMUEL–KINGS
· · · · · · · · · · · · ·

We have reunited the four books of 1 Samuel, 2 Samuel, 1 Kings, and 2 Kings that were separated because they were too long to fit on one scroll. Together they tell the single story of the Israelite monarchy from beginning to end—the final chronicle of the Covenant History, which is built out of the list of Israel's kings. Spanning several centuries, Samuel–Kings describes the reigns of the kings who presided over the united nation, and then the kingdoms of Israel and Judah it was divided into. The kings are evaluated by the standard of wholehearted dedication to God set by David, so one after another we see whether or not a king *did what was right in the eyes of the* Lord, *just as his father David had done.*

What to watch for in Samuel–Kings: Although the kings of Israel and Judah practically drill Israel into oblivion because they aren't faithful to God, look for the glimmer of hope that emerges from their place of exile in Babylon at the conclusion of this book.

 PERSONAL BIBLE EXPERIENCE

Your personal Bible experience starts with a daily practice of reading the Bible. This week before your group meeting, read the books of Ruth and the first part of Samuel–Kings. Use the journaling space to capture your thoughts, questions, responses, emotions, and insights as you read the daily selection. Keep in mind the questions you will be talking about with your discussion group:

- What was new or compelling to you?
- What questions did you have?
- Was there anything that bothered you?
- What did you learn about loving God?
- What did you learn about loving others?

Daily Reading Journal

Day 26: Ruth Invitation–4:22 (pages 389–396)

_____

_____

_____

_____

_____

_____

Day 27: Samuel–Kings Invitation–1 Samuel 12:25 (pages 397–415)

_____

_____

_____

_____

_____

_____

Day 28: 1 Samuel 13:1–18:4 (pages 415–426)

_____

_____

_____

_____

_____

_____

Day 29: 1 Samuel 18:5–24:22 (pages 426–436)

_____

_____

_____

_____

_____

_____

Day 30: 1 Samuel 25:1–2 Samuel 5:3 (pages 436–452)

_____

_____

_____

_____

_____

_____

 **COMMUNITY BIBLE EXPERIENCE**

Welcome to Session 6 of the Community Bible Experience. You have been experiencing the Bible personally by reading through the books of Ruth and Samuel–Kings this week, and now your group has gathered to experience the Bible in community with each other. Think of your discussion as more of a book club than a Bible study.

Reflecting on the Previous Week (30–60 minutes)

From your Personal Bible Experience in Ruth and the first part of Samuel–Kings this week, have a conversation with your group about what you read by answering the following questions.

What was new or compelling to you?

What questions did you have?

Was there anything that bothered you?

What did you learn about loving God?

What did you learn about loving others?

Preparing for the Week Ahead (15–20 minutes)

WATCH VIDEO WEEK 7: SAMUEL–KINGS

To get the most out of what you will be reading in the coming week, close your time together by watching the video of Bible teacher John Walton explaining the themes and relevance of the next part of Samuel–Kings. Use the following outline to jot down any additional insights or questions.

VIDEO NOTES

2 Samuel 5:4–1 Kings 14:31

Point of Samuel

David is the rightful king by God's choice.

God's covenant with David

David's troubles move toward a split kingdom.

Themes of Samuel

Ark of the covenant

Kingship

Davidic Covenant

Assessing Saul as the people's choice, with his failures

Assessing David as God's choice, with his failures

Overview of 1 Kings 1–14

Solomon's movement to the throne

Covers Solomon to Rehoboam, 970–930 BC

Themes of 1 Kings

Temple

Solomon's wisdom

Solomon's wives

Division of the kingdom and golden calves

Relevance of Samuel–Kings

God's progressive dwelling among his people

God works through flawed kings.

God's plans and purposes are carried out even when the kings are unfaithful.

THIS WEEK
· · · · · · · · · ·

Read the next part of Samuel–Kings in *The Books of the Bible, Covenant History.* Maintain your momentum by keeping these guidelines in mind:

- Read what you can.
- Read something every day.
- Always have your *Books of the Bible* with you.
- Every week is a new week.
- Use this study journal as you do your reading for Week 7: Samuel–Kings, recording any thoughts on the Daily Reading Journal pages.

WEEK 7
SAMUEL–KINGS

PERSONAL BIBLE EXPERIENCE

Your personal Bible experience starts with a daily practice of reading the Bible. This week before your group meeting, read the next part of Samuel–Kings. Use the journaling space to capture your thoughts, questions, responses, emotions, and insights as you read the daily selection. Keep in mind the questions you will be talking about with your discussion group:

- What was new or compelling to you?
- What questions did you have?
- Was there anything that bothered you?
- What did you learn about loving God?
- What did you learn about loving others?

Daily Reading Journal

Day 31: 2 Samuel 5:4–14:33 (pages 452–467)

_____

_____

_____

_____

_____

Day 32: 2 Samuel 15:1–20:25 (pages 467–478)

_____

_____

_____

_____

_____

Day 33: 2 Samuel 21:1–1 Kings 2:12 (pages 478–491)

_____

_____

_____

_____

Day 34: 1 Kings 2:13–7:51 (pages 491–502)

_____

_____

_____

_____

Day 35: 1 Kings 8:1–14:20 (pages 502–516)

_____

_____

_____

_____

COMMUNITY BIBLE EXPERIENCE

Welcome to Session 7 of the Community Bible Experience. You have been experiencing the Bible personally by reading through the next part of Samuel–Kings this week, and now your group has gathered to experience the Bible in community with each other. Think of your discussion as more of a book club than a Bible study.

Reflecting on the Previous Week (30–60 minutes)

From your Personal Bible Experience in Samuel–Kings this week, have a conversation with your group about what you read by answering the following questions.

What was new or compelling to you?

What questions did you have?

Was there anything that bothered you?

What did you learn about loving God?

What did you learn about loving others?

Preparing for the Week Ahead (15–20 minutes)

WATCH VIDEO WEEK 8: SAMUEL–KINGS
· ·

To get the most out of what you will be reading in the coming week, close
your time together by watching the video of Bible teacher John Walton
explaining the themes and relevance of the last part of Samuel–Kings.
Use the following outline to jot down any additional insights or questions.

VIDEO NOTES

The Divided Kingdom

Purpose of Kings

Litany of failure: Not to give us history, but theology—to know God, his plans, and his purposes

God's kingship is revealed regardless of individual kings.

Role of prophets

God provides for Israel, not Baal.

Relevance of Kings

God is patient with his people through times when leadership is inadequate.

[Jeroboam II] did evil in the eyes of the LORD and did not turn away from any of the sins of Jeroboam son of Nebat, which he had caused Israel to commit. He was the one who restored the boundaries of Israel from Lebo Hamath to the Dead Sea, in accordance with the word of the LORD, the God of Israel, spoken through his servant Jonah son of Amittai, the prophet from Gath Hepher. The LORD had seen how bitterly everyone in Israel, whether slave or free, was suffering; there was no one to help them. And since the LORD had not said he would blot out the name of Israel from under heaven, he saved them by the hand of Jeroboam son of Jehoash.

(2 KINGS 14:24–27)

God has grace and compassion as he carries out his purposes.

THIS WEEK
· · · · · · · · · ·

Read the last part of Samuel–Kings in *The Books of the Bible, Covenant History.* Maintain your momentum by keeping these guidelines in mind:

- Read what you can.
- Read something every day.
- Always have your *Books of the Bible* with you.
- Every week is a new week.
- Use this study journal as you do your reading for Week 8: Samuel–Kings, recording any thoughts on the Daily Reading Journal pages.

WEEK 8

SAMUEL–KINGS

PERSONAL BIBLE EXPERIENCE

Your personal Bible experience starts with a daily practice of reading the Bible. This week before your group meeting, read the last part of Samuel–Kings. Use the journaling space to capture your thoughts, questions, responses, emotions, and insights as you read the daily selection. Keep in mind the questions you will be talking about with your discussion group:

- What was new or compelling to you?
- What questions did you have?
- Was there anything that bothered you?
- What did you learn about loving God?
- What did you learn about loving others?

Daily Reading Journal

Day 36: 1 Kings 14:21–22:40 (pages 516–533)

_____

_____

_____

_____

Day 37: 1 Kings 22:41–2 Kings 8:15 (pages 533–547)

_____

_____

_____

_____

Day 38: 2 Kings 8:16–14:22 (pages 547–559)

_____

_____

_____

_____

_____

Day 39: 2 Kings 14:23–20:21 (pages 559–572)

_____

_____

_____

_____

_____

Day 40: 2 Kings 21:1–25:30 (pages 572–581)

_____

_____

_____

_____

_____

COMMUNITY BIBLE EXPERIENCE

Welcome to Session 8 of the Community Bible Experience. You have been experiencing the Bible personally by reading through the last part of Samuel–Kings this week, and now your group has gathered to experience the Bible in community with each other. Think of your discussion as more of a book club than a Bible study.

Reflecting on the Previous Week (30–60 minutes)

From your Personal Bible Experience in Samuel–Kings this week, have a conversation with your group about what you read by answering the following questions.

What was new or compelling to you?

What questions did you have?

Was there anything that bothered you?

What did you learn about loving God?

What did you learn about loving others?

Final Reflections (15–30 minutes)

Reflect: Give each person a chance to share how their journey through the Covenant History impacted them, how it shaped their understanding of the Bible, and what implications it might have for their life.

Rejoice: Celebrate your achievement together! Reading through *The Books of the Bible, Covenant History* in just eight weeks is a major accomplishment.

Regroup: Plan your next meeting.

If you are taking a break before you start the next volume of *The Books of the Bible*, choose the date for your introductory session. To whet your appetite for what's next, read the Invitation to the Prophets on page 73 of this journal.

If you are continuing to *The Books of the Bible, The Prophets* next week, go ahead and watch the video of Bible teacher John Walton explaining the indictment, judgment, instruction, aftermath, and relevance of Jonah, Amos, Hosea, Micah, and Isaiah 1–5, and take notes on pages 76–79 of this journal.

God's covenant spokesmen,

HIS SERVANTS THE PROPHETS,

bring the word of the Lord

TO HIS PEOPLE ISRAEL,

announcing a message

OF CLEANSING JUDGMENT

AS WELL AS HOPE AND RENEWAL

for all of God's good creation.

INVITATION TO
THE PROPHETS

The books of the prophets make up the second major division of the First Testament. These books account for about one quarter of the whole Bible and are presented in what is plausibly their historical order. The prophets were people chosen by God over a 300-year period to bring the word of the Lord to Israel at urgent times in the life of that nation. Though they came from many different walks of life and lived under different historical conditions, the prophets nevertheless speak with a single voice.

The foundation of everything the prophets said was the covenant bond between Israel and the Lord. The essential theme of their message, which can be seen in the actual sequence of oracles built into many of the prophetic books, is first judgment on the house of Israel for the failure to follow God's ways, then judgment on the other nations, and finally a promise of future restoration and hope.

Many of the prophets speak of a hope that lies beyond these prophetic books, beyond the First Testament itself. This is a hope for a grand and universal salvation that extends beyond Israel, to the nations of the world and finally even to the creation itself. All things will be made new. The prophets looked to later events concerning one who will take Israel's suffering and exile onto himself, facing the crisis of judgment to find vindication for a renewed Israel in the surprising ways of their faithful God.

INTRODUCTORY SESSION

The Introductory Session introduces your group to *The Books of the Bible, The Prophets*. Hold the Introductory Session the week before your first meeting. If you are reading straight through all four volumes, you will only hold one Introductory Session, which will take place before you begin your first volume. If you are spreading out your reading of the four volumes, it is helpful to have an introductory gathering the week before you start each one.

Getting to Know You (15–30 minutes)

If your group is new to each other, or if you have any new members in your group for this session, invite each group member to introduce themselves, using any or all of the following prompts:

- List three of your roles in life and what you like about them.
- What one word describes your past experience of reading the Bible?
- What do you hope to get from this journey of reading *The Books of the Bible, The Prophets* together?

Introduction (15–30 minutes)

INTRODUCE THE
COMMUNITY BIBLE EXPERIENCE

Explain how the Community Bible Experience works by summarizing the information in the book introduction, starting on page 7 of this study journal. The key points are:

- Five tips for Bible reading
- Weekly reading plan
- Weekly discussion questions for groups
- Three tips for weekly gatherings

Allow time for discussion about how your group wants to function with each other and to address any concerns people have about doing the Bible reading.

INTRODUCE *THE PROPHETS*

The Books of the Bible, The Prophets contains six sections of important introductory material. If time allows, read through all six sections of the introductory material together. If your group has read other volumes in the past, or if you have time constraints, focus on the Drama of the Bible in Six Acts, page iii (it's helpful to read that together before every new series), and read the Invitation to the Prophets, page xiv.

Preparing for the Week Ahead (15–20 minutes)

Discuss the challenge of reading 12 pages a day. Remind participants that most readings take around 30 minutes to complete—about the same time it takes to watch a short TV show.

WATCH VIDEO WEEK 1:
JONAH, AMOS, HOSEA, MICAH, ISAIAH

To get the most out of what you will be reading in the coming week, close your time together by watching the video of Bible teacher John Walton explaining the indictment, judgment, instruction, aftermath, and relevance of Jonah, Amos, Hosea, Micah, and Isaiah 1–5. Use the following outline to jot down any additional insights or questions.

VIDEO NOTES

How to Read the Prophets

Focus on the message the prophet had for his audience.

Jonah (during Jeroboam II, 8th century)

Nineveh and Assyrians were not a threat to Israel at the time.

Jonah's message is judgment, not repentance or conversion.

Themes of Jonah

Jonah's reluctance and anger

If God can show compassion to Nineveh, he can show compassion to his people.

Important introduction to the prophets: Their point is that God wants small steps in the right direction.

Amos (760 BC, to Israel)

Classical prophets begin speaking to the people, rather than to kings.

Indictment: Social injustice and empty rituals

Judgment: Overrun by an enemy and destruction

Instruction: Do justice.

Aftermath: Restoration

Relevance: Judgment is possible for God's people.

Hosea (contemporary of Amos, to Israel)

Indictment: Unfaithfulness and syncretism

Judgment: Covenant blessings and protection retracted

Instruction: Acknowledge guilt, seek the Lord, and return to the Lord.

Aftermath: God's faithfulness can be restored.

Relevance: God is faithful even when his people are not; this is a reason for hope.

Micah (contemporary of Isaiah, during Assyrian crisis, to Judah)

Indictment: Injustice and idolatry

Judgment: Destruction and exile

Instruction: Do justice.

Aftermath: Return of remnant, peace, and reign of God

Relevance: What does the Lord require? To act like God's people.

Isaiah 1–5 (contemporary of Micah, during Assyrian crisis)

Overture: Israel as God's vineyard

Indictment: Trusting others rather than the Lord; appalling worship practices

Judgment: Deliverance into the hands of the Assyrians

Instruction: Trust, purify, repent, and return to the Lord.

Aftermath: Political and spiritual restoration; coming messianic king

Relevance: Day of the Lord is coming; so is restoration.

THIS WEEK

Read the books of Jonah, Amos, Hosea, Micah, and Isaiah 1–5 in *The Books of the Bible, The Prophets*. Maintain your momentum by keeping these guidelines in mind:

- Read what you can.
- Read something every day.
- Always have your *Books of the Bible* with you.
- Every week is a new week.
- Use this study journal as you do your reading for Week 1: Jonah, Amos, Hosea, Micah, Isaiah, recording any thoughts on the Daily Journal Reading pages.

WEEK 1
JONAH, AMOS, HOSEA, MICAH, ISAIAH

JONAH

The prophet Jonah seems to represent the attitude many people in Israel took at various times toward other nations. Instead of recognizing their mission to be God's agent for bringing blessing to the world, they considered other nations their enemies and expected God to destroy them. God's question to Jonah at the end of the book—*Should I not have concern for the great city of Nineveh?*—is also being posed to any readers who share Jonah's hostile attitude to foreigners.

What to watch for in Jonah: Of all the people and things mentioned in the book—the storm, the sailors, the fish, a Gentile nation, the plant, etc.—only the prophet himself fails to obey God. Observe how God uses all these elements to teach Jonah a lesson in compassion and obedience.

AMOS

Amos was a shepherd-turned-prophet who used oracles, sermons, visions, and promises to try to get the Northern Kingdom of Israel to stop their hypocritical religiosity and thereby avoid God's judgment.

What to watch for in Amos: After all the harsh judgments, Amos proclaims some of the greatest prophecies of restoration for Israel anywhere in Scripture (see page 23).

HOSEA

More than any other prophet, Hosea's personal experiences illustrate his prophetic message. Instructed by God to marry Gomer, Hosea (a name derived from the same Hebrew root word as Joshua and Jesus) finds his domestic life to be an accurate and tragic dramatization of the spiritual adultery of the Northern Kingdom of Israel.

What to watch for in Hosea: See how loyal, unconditional, and ceaseless God's love is.

MICAH

Micah, himself from a small country village, stands against the injustices of his day as the prophet of the downtrodden and exploited people of the Southern Kingdom of Judah. Interestingly, it is Micah who predicts Jesus's birth in Bethlehem.

What to watch for in Micah: This prophet emphasizes the fundamental relationship between true spirituality and social justice.

ISAIAH

Called the "St. Paul of the Old Testament," Isaiah was from an educated and distinguished Jewish family. His prophetic ministry in the Southern Kingdom of Judah spanned the reigns of four kings. His messianic prophecies are clearer and more explicit than any other Old Testament book.

What to watch for in Isaiah: The name Isaiah means "Salvation is of the Lord," and salvation happens to be the theme of the book. The word *salvation* appears twenty-six times in Isaiah, but only seven times in all the other prophets combined.

PERSONAL BIBLE EXPERIENCE

Your personal Bible experience starts with a daily practice of reading the Bible. This week before your group meeting, read the books of Jonah, Amos, Hosea, Micah, and the beginning of Isaiah. Use the journaling space to capture your thoughts, questions, responses, emotions, and insights as you read the daily selection. Keep in mind the questions you will be talking about with your discussion group:

- What was new or compelling to you?
- What questions did you have?
- Was there anything that bothered you?
- What did you learn about loving God?
- What did you learn about loving others?

Daily Reading Journal

Day 1: Jonah Invitation–Amos 2:16 (pages 1–12)

_____

_____

_____

_____

_____

Day 2: Amos 3:1–Hosea 3:5 (pages 12–34)

_____

_____

_____

_____

_____

Day 3: Hosea 4:1–14:9 (pages 34–51)

_____

_____

_____

_____

_____

Day 4: Micah Invitation–7:20 (pages 53–67)

_____

_____

_____

_____

_____

Day 5: Isaiah Invitation–5:30 (pages 69–84)

_____

_____

_____

_____

_____

 **COMMUNITY BIBLE EXPERIENCE**

Welcome to Session 1 of the Community Bible Experience. You have been experiencing the Bible personally by reading through the books of Jonah, Amos, Hosea, Micah, and the beginning of Isaiah this week, and now your group has gathered to experience the Bible in community with each other. Think of your discussion as more of a book club than a Bible study.

Reflecting on the Previous Week (30–60 minutes)

From your Personal Bible Experience in the books of Jonah, Amos, Hosea, Micah, and Isaiah this week, have a conversation with your group about what you read by answering the following questions.

What was new or compelling to you?

What questions did you have?

Was there anything that bothered you?

What did you learn about loving God?

What did you learn about loving others?

Preparing for the Week Ahead (15–20 minutes)

WATCH VIDEO WEEK 2: ISAIAH

To get the most out of what you will be reading in the coming week, close your time together by watching the video of Bible teacher John Walton explaining the themes and relevance of Isaiah 6–44. Use the following outline to jot down any additional insights or questions.

VIDEO NOTES

Prophets do not predict the future but proclaim the plan of God.

Prophets are champions of the covenant.

Historical Context of Isaiah

Syro-Ephraimite War and King Ahaz

Assyrian Sennacherib's invasion

When Hezekiah trusts God, the Assyrians are defeated.

Shift at Isaiah 40: Isaiah is speaking to exiles in the Babylonian crisis.

Themes of Isaiah

Trusting God

Sons' names as signs

Immanuel theology

God's plans in both present and future

God as Redeemer from crises

Holy One of Israel

Relevance of Isaiah

There is an inclination of God's people to not listen; consequently, we are not fully participating in God's purposes.

THIS WEEK

Read Isaiah 6–44 in *The Books of the Bible, The Prophets*. Maintain your momentum by keeping these guidelines in mind:

- Read what you can.
- Read something every day.
- Always have your *Books of the Bible* with you.
- Every week is a new week.
- Use this study journal as you do your reading for Week 2: Isaiah, recording any thoughts on the Daily Reading Journal pages.

WEEK 2
ISAIAH

PERSONAL BIBLE EXPERIENCE

Your personal Bible experience starts with a daily practice of reading the Bible. This week before your group meeting, read Isaiah 6–44. Use the journaling space to capture your thoughts, questions, responses, emotions, and insights as you read the daily selection. Keep in mind the questions you will be talking about with your discussion group:

- What was new or compelling to you?
- What questions did you have?
- Was there anything that bothered you?
- What did you learn about loving God?
- What did you learn about loving others?

Daily Reading Journal

Day 6: Isaiah 6:1–12:6 (pages 84–96)

_____
_____
_____
_____
_____

Day 7: Isaiah 13:1–23:18 (pages 96–115)

_____
_____
_____
_____
_____

Day 8: Isaiah 24:1–33:24 (pages 115–136)

_____

_____

_____

_____

_____

Day 9: Isaiah 34:1–39:8 (pages 136–146)

_____

_____

_____

_____

Day 10: Isaiah 40:1–44:23 (pages 146–160)

_____

_____

_____

_____

 **COMMUNITY BIBLE EXPERIENCE**

Welcome to Session 2 of the Community Bible Experience. You have been experiencing the Bible personally by reading through a portion of the book of Isaiah this week, and now your group has gathered to experience the Bible in community with each other. Think of your discussion as more of a book club than a Bible study.

Reflecting on the Previous Week (30–60 minutes)

From your Personal Bible Experience in Isaiah this week, have a conversation with your group about what you read by answering the following questions.

What was new or compelling to you?

What questions did you have?

Was there anything that bothered you?

What did you learn about loving God?

What did you learn about loving others?

Preparing for the Week Ahead (15–20 minutes)

WATCH VIDEO WEEK 3: ISAIAH, ZEPHANIAH, NAHUM, HABAKKUK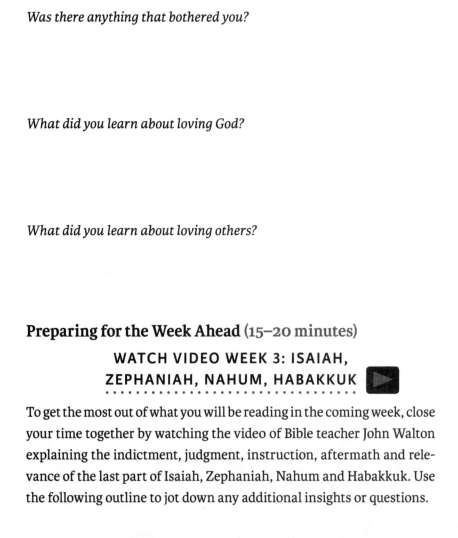

To get the most out of what you will be reading in the coming week, close your time together by watching the video of Bible teacher John Walton explaining the indictment, judgment, instruction, aftermath and relevance of the last part of Isaiah, Zephaniah, Nahum and Habakkuk. Use the following outline to jot down any additional insights or questions.

VIDEO NOTES

Isaiah 45–66 (Babylonian crisis and post-exilic crisis)

The prophets' message had relevance to the original audience; they were not given information about the fulfillment of their message.

Highlights of Isaiah

Isaiah 53: Substitute king ritual

Isaiah 58: Fasting and Sabbath—these rituals were focused on turning our attention to God's kingdom.

Themes of Isaiah

Uniqueness of the God of Israel

Plans for the future

Servant of Yahweh

God's thoughts and ways are not ours.

New heavens and new earth

Relevance of Isaiah

God has compassion on his people.

Long-term working out of God's plans and purposes

Zephaniah (connected to Josiah's reforms, contemporary with Jeremiah, transition from Assyrian to Babylonian crisis)

Indictment: Pagan worship

Judgment: Destruction given in universal terms

Instruction: Seek the Lord.

Aftermath: Remnant will be left, gathering of oppressed, and God's kingship

Relevance: A day is coming when the scales will be balanced; restoration of remnant

Nahum (before Zephaniah, approximately 655 BC, 100 years after Jonah, to Nineveh)

Indictment: None

Judgment: Fall of Nineveh

Instruction: None

Aftermath: Hope for restoration for Judah

Relevance: Empires fall in their time; a call to trust God

Habakkuk (contemporary of Jeremiah and Josiah, 7th century)

Problem: Judah is just as bad as before judgment. "How can you use those even more wicked to bring about justice?"

Response: Habakkuk's hymn (chapter 3) declares God as judge and deliverer; response of trust

Indictment: Judah's injustice, Babylon's violence, bloodshed, and oppression

Judgment: Judah will have the Babylonian invasion; Babylon will be victimized, shamed.

Instruction: Live faithfully.

Aftermath: None

Relevance: God uses whom he will to bring judgment; his people have a responsibility for faithfulness even in hard times.

THIS WEEK

· · · · · · · · · ·

Read the last part of Isaiah and the books of Zephaniah, Nahum, and Habakkuk in *The Books of the Bible, The Prophets*. Maintain your momentum by keeping these guidelines in mind:

- Read what you can.
- Read something every day.
- Always have your *Books of the Bible* with you.
- Every week is a new week.
- Use this study journal as you do your reading for Week 3: Isaiah, Zephaniah, Nahum, Habakkuk, recording any thoughts on the Daily Reading Journal pages.

WEEK 3
ISAIAH, ZEPHANIAH, NAHUM, HABAKKUK

ZEPHANIAH

As the only prophet descended from royalty (and in fact descended from godly King Hezekiah), Zephaniah was effective in influencing young King Josiah to depart from the evil ways of his father and grandfather and establish reforms that led to a spiritual revival.

What to watch for in Zephaniah: Look for all the references to the "day of the Lord," where Judah, all the surrounding nations, and in the future the whole earth will be judged.

NAHUM

Unlike Jonah one hundred years before him, Nahum does not go to the city of Nineveh but declares his oracle from afar. This time, Nineveh will not respond to God's message with humility and repentance, thereby escaping destruction. Rather, as they amass the most power of any empire in the world, their arrogance and wickedness seal their doom.

What to watch for in Nahum: Nahum reminds Nineveh of other nations whose arrogance made them feel invincible, calling to mind the warning from the apostle Paul, "Let him who thinks he stands take heed lest he fall" (1 Corinthians 10:12).

HABAKKUK

This prophet, who appears to be the equivalent of our modern-day worship leader, asks God a universal question: Why do bad things happen to comparatively good people? God's answer doesn't make him feel any better.

What to watch for in Habakkuk: After wrestling with how God plans to deal with Judah, Habakkuk's final declaration of joy in spite of apparent circumstances is one of the most majestic in all of Scripture.

 **PERSONAL BIBLE EXPERIENCE**

Your personal Bible experience starts with a daily practice of reading the Bible. This week before your group meeting, read the rest of Isaiah and the books Zephaniah, Nahum, and Habakkuk. Use the journaling space to capture your thoughts, questions, responses, emotions, and insights as you read the daily selection. Keep in mind the questions you will be talking about with your discussion group:

- What was new or compelling to you?
- What questions did you have?
- Was there anything that bothered you?
- What did you learn about loving God?
- What did you learn about loving others?

Daily Reading Journal

Day 11: Isaiah 44:24–49:26 (pages 160–172)

_____

_____

_____

_____

_____

Day 12: Isaiah 50:1–55:13 (pages 173–183)

_____

_____

_____

_____

Day 13: Isaiah 56:1–61:11 (pages 183–195)

_____

_____

_____

_____

_____

Day 14: Isaiah 62:1–66:24 (pages 195–205)

_____

_____

_____

_____

_____

Day 15: Zephaniah Invitation–Habakkuk 3:19 (pages 207–232)

_____

_____

_____

_____

_____

 **COMMUNITY BIBLE EXPERIENCE**

Welcome to Session 3 of the Community Bible Experience. You have been experiencing the Bible personally by reading through the books of Isaiah, Zephaniah, Nahum, and Habakkuk this week, and now your group has gathered to experience the Bible in community with each other. Think of your discussion as more of a book club than a Bible study.

Reflecting on the Previous Week (30–60 minutes)

From your Personal Bible Experience in the books of Isaiah, Zephaniah, Nahum, and Habakkuk this week, have a conversation with your group about what you read by answering the following questions.

What was new or compelling to you?

What questions did you have?

Was there anything that bothered you?

What did you learn about loving God?

What did you learn about loving others?

Preparing for the Week Ahead (15–20 minutes)

WATCH VIDEO WEEK 4: JEREMIAH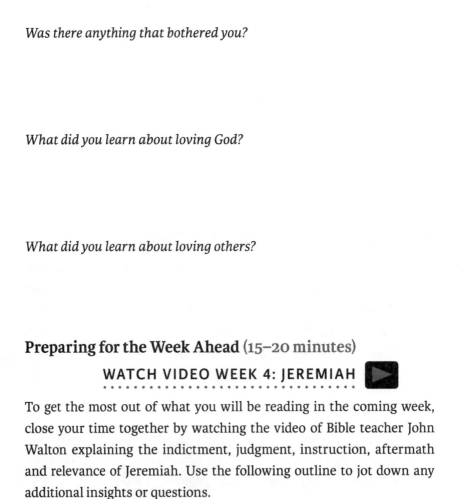

To get the most out of what you will be reading in the coming week, close your time together by watching the video of Bible teacher John Walton explaining the indictment, judgment, instruction, aftermath and relevance of Jeremiah. Use the following outline to jot down any additional insights or questions.

VIDEO NOTES

Jeremiah

Historical Background of Jeremiah

627 BC—Jeremiah called as a prophet

628 BC—Josiah's first reform begins.

627 BC—Assyria begins to lose power; death of Ashurbanipal

626 BC—Babylon's power begins to rise.

"See, today I appoint you over the nations and kingdoms to uproot and tear down, to destroy and overthrow, to build and to plant" (Jeremiah 1:10).

Mission of Jeremiah

Called to be the champion of the covenant

Temple sermon (Jeremiah 7, 26): Addresses the mishandling and misunderstanding of God's presence

Face false prophets

Indictment: Treachery in forsaking the Lord and the covenant

Judgment: Enemy from the north

Instruction: Repent

Aftermath: New Covenant; return from exile

Relevance: Worthlessness of idols; God shapes his people as he will; God is angered by the hypocrisy of his people regarding his presence

THIS WEEK

Read the first half of the book of Jeremiah in *The Books of the Bible, The Prophets*. Maintain your momentum by keeping these guidelines in mind:

- Read what you can.
- Read something every day.
- Always have your *Books of the Bible* with you.
- Every week is a new week.
- Use this study journal as you do your reading for Week 4: Jeremiah, recording any thoughts on the Daily Reading Journal page.

WEEK 4
JEREMIAH

JEREMIAH

Known as the "weeping prophet," this son of a priest spent forty years as a much-maligned prophet proclaiming doom to the stubborn people of Judah. God spoke through Jeremiah using oracles, prophecies, sermons, parables, his tears, and most striking of all, object lessons.

What to watch for in Jeremiah: Jeremiah is a heartbroken man who lets us glimpse into his intimate relationship with God as he processes his questions, his protests, and his anguish.

 ### PERSONAL BIBLE EXPERIENCE

Your personal Bible experience starts with a daily practice of reading the Bible. This week before your group meeting, read the first half of the book of Jeremiah. Use the journaling space to capture your thoughts, questions, responses, emotions, and insights as you read the daily selection. Keep in mind the questions you will be talking about with your discussion group:

- What was new or compelling to you?
- What questions did you have?
- Was there anything that bothered you?
- What did you learn about loving God?
- What did you learn about loving others?

Daily Reading Journal

Day 16: Jeremiah Invitation–3:5 (pages 233–243)

_____

_____

_____

_____

_____

Day 17: Jeremiah 3:6–6:30 (pages 243–255)

_____

_____

_____

_____

_____

Day 18: Jeremiah 7:1–12:17 (pages 255–268)

_____

_____

_____

_____

_____

Day 19: Jeremiah 13:1–17:27 (pages 268–278)

_____

_____

_____

_____

_____

Day 20: Jeremiah 18:1–25:14 (pages 279–292)

_____

_____

_____

_____

_____

 **COMMUNITY BIBLE EXPERIENCE**

Welcome to Session 4 of the Community Bible Experience. You have been experiencing the Bible personally by reading through the first half of the book of Jeremiah this week, and now your group has gathered to experience the Bible in community with each other. Think of your discussion as more of a book club than a Bible study.

Reflecting on the Previous Week (30–60 minutes)

From your Personal Bible Experience in Jeremiah this week, have a conversation with your group about what you read by answering the following questions.

What was new or compelling to you?

What questions did you have?

Was there anything that bothered you?

What did you learn about loving God?

What did you learn about loving others?

Preparing for the Week Ahead (15–20 minutes)

WATCH VIDEO WEEK 5: JEREMIAH 26–52

To get the most out of what you will be reading in the coming week, close your time together by watching the video of Bible teacher John Walton explaining the themes and relevance of Jeremiah 26–52. Use the following outline to jot down any additional insights or questions.

VIDEO NOTES

Overview of Jeremiah 26–52

Jeremiah's increased persecution

Prophesies destruction of Jerusalem by Babylonians

Prophesies 70 years of exile

Includes "Book of Consolation"—God is not done with Israel.

Some flee to Egypt in self-protection.

Recounts the fall of Jerusalem

Themes of Jeremiah

New Covenant

Abrahamic Covenant—God dwelling among his people

Davidic Covenant—God ruling over his people

Sinaic Covenant—How to live in God's presence

Land, Torah, God's presence, David's line

People are a light to the nations.

Writes the Torah on heart, not internalizing the Torah but using
   Israel as his revelation

Forgiveness

Relevance

God is committed to reestablishing his presence.

God is willing to respond dramatically to unfaithfulness.

THIS WEEK

Read the rest of the book of Jeremiah in *The Books of the Bible, The Prophets*. Maintain your momentum by keeping these guidelines in mind:

- Read what you can.
- Read something every day.
- Always have your *Books of the Bible* with you.
- Every week is a new week.
- Use this study journal as you do your reading for Week 5: Jeremiah, recording any thoughts on the Daily Reading Journal pages.

WEEK 5
JEREMIAH

PERSONAL BIBLE EXPERIENCE

Your personal Bible experience starts with a daily practice of reading the Bible. This week before your group meeting, read the rest of the book of Jeremiah. Use the journaling space to capture your thoughts, questions, responses, emotions, and insights as you read the daily selection. Keep in mind the questions you will be talking about with your discussion group:

- What was new or compelling to you?
- What questions did you have?
- Was there anything that bothered you?
- What did you learn about loving God?
- What did you learn about loving others?

Daily Reading Journal

Day 21: Jeremiah 25:15–31:40 (pages 292–306)

_____

_____

_____

_____

_____

Day 22: Jeremiah 32:1–36:32 (pages 307–315)

_____

_____

_____

_____

Day 23: Jeremiah 37:1–45:5 (pages 315–326)

_____

_____

_____

_____

_____

Day 24: Jeremiah 46:1–49:39 (pages 326–339)

_____

_____

_____

_____

_____

Day 25: Jeremiah 50:1–52:34 (pages 340–354)

_____

_____

_____

_____

_____

COMMUNITY BIBLE EXPERIENCE

Welcome to Session 5 of the Community Bible Experience. You have been experiencing the Bible personally by reading through the rest of the book of Jeremiah this week, and now your group has gathered to experience the Bible in community with each other. Think of your discussion as more of a book club than a Bible study.

Reflecting on the Previous Week (30–60 minutes)

From your Personal Bible Experience in Jeremiah this week, have a conversation with your group about what you read by answering the following questions.

What was new or compelling to you?

What questions did you have?

Was there anything that bothered you?

What did you learn about loving God?

What did you learn about loving others?

Preparing for the Week Ahead (15–20 minutes)

WATCH VIDEO WEEK 6: OBADIAH, EZEKIEL 1–24

To get the most out of what you will be reading in the coming week, close your time together by watching the video of Bible teacher John Walton explaining the indictment, judgment, instruction, aftermath, and relevance of Obadiah and Ezekiel 1–24. Use the following outline to jot down any additional insights or questions.

VIDEO NOTES

Obadiah (to Edom)

Indictment: Mistreatment of Judah

Judgment: Edom's destruction

Instruction: None

Aftermath: Deliverance for Israel

Theme: Day of the Lord

Relevance: God holds nations responsible for how they treat his people.

Ezekiel (contemporary of Jeremiah, in exile in Babylon, called to prophesy about Jerusalem in 593 BC)

Eat the scroll.

Ezekiel 3:3

Overview of Ezekiel

Elaborated visions

He sees the throne in his commissioning (Ezekiel 1).

He is transported to Jerusalem (Ezekiel 8–11)

Seven sign acts; eight allegories

Indictment: Israel's unfaithfulness and injustice

Judgment: Jerusalem will be abandoned and destroyed.

Instruction: Repent; do justice.

Themes: Ezekiel as a watchman; departure of God's presence
   (Ezekiel 10)

Relevance: God will never leave us or forsake us, yet he may
   abandon his people to the consequences of their bad choices.

THIS WEEK

Read the book of Obadiah and the first part of Ezekiel in *The Books of
the Bible, The Prophets*. Maintain your momentum by keeping these
guidelines in mind:

- Read what you can.
- Read something every day.
- Always have your *Books of the Bible* with you.
- Every week is a new week.
- Use this study journal as you do your reading for Week 6:
  Obadiah, Ezekiel, recording any thoughts on the Daily Reading
  Journal pages.

OBADIAH

This, the shortest book in the First Testament, packs the biggest punch. Obadiah carries one of the strongest messages of judgment in the First Testament. Edom, the nation descended from Jacob's twin brother Esau, will be completely annihilated—no survivors, no chance of changing God's mind—because they gloated over the invasion of Jerusalem. This is the same Edom who refused passage through their mountainous land to the Israelites on their way to Canaan. An enmity that started in the womb will be carried to a disastrous conclusion.

What to watch for in Obadiah: Think about how important it is to live a life of no regrets. The way you conduct yourself with your family has a generational impact.

EZEKIEL

This priestly prophet goes to extreme and shocking lengths to proclaim God's message of judgment to the Jewish exiles in Babylon. He enacts a series of human object lessons that call to mind brutal prisoner-of-war tortures to demonstrate the judgment coming to the city of Jerusalem and to the kingdoms of Israel and Judah. He uses dramatic signs, striking parables, powerful sermons, and damning oracles to proclaim God's messages to Judah as well as to the surrounding Gentile nations. His vivid visions, most famously the vision of the dry bones, both strike terror and inspire awe. His detailed description of the restored temple clearly connects back to the original glory of the Garden of Eden, where the most glorious and wonderful feature is God's presence. In fact, Ezekiel ends his book with the new name of the new Jerusalem, "THE LORD IS THERE."

What to watch for in Ezekiel: God's presence brings restoration. Look for what happens when God's presence is removed, compared to when his presence returns, as illustrated by this statement: *"I will give you a new heart and put a new spirit in you; I will remove from you your heart of stone and give you a heart of flesh"* (page 425).

PERSONAL BIBLE EXPERIENCE

Your personal Bible experience starts with a daily practice of reading the Bible. This week before your group meeting, read the books of Obadiah and the first part of Ezekiel. Use the journaling space to capture your thoughts, questions, responses, emotions, and insights as you read the daily selection. Keep in mind the questions you will be talking about with your discussion group:

- What was new or compelling to you?
- What questions did you have?
- Was there anything that bothered you?
- What did you learn about loving God?
- What did you learn about loving others?

Daily Reading Journal

Day 26: Obadiah Invitation–Ezekiel 3:15 (pages 355–368)

_____

_____

_____

_____

_____

Day 27: Ezekiel 3:16–11:25 (pages 368–378)

_____

_____

_____

_____

_____

Day 28: Ezekiel 12:1–16:63 (pages 378–386)

_____

_____

_____

_____

_____

Day 29: Ezekiel 17:1–21:32 (pages 386–397)

_____

_____

_____

_____

_____

Day 30: Ezekiel 22:1–24:27 (pages 397–403)

_____

_____

_____

_____

_____

 **COMMUNITY BIBLE EXPERIENCE**

Welcome to Session 6 of the Community Bible Experience. You have been experiencing the Bible personally by reading through the books of Obadiah and the first part of Ezekiel this week, and now your group has gathered to experience the Bible in community with each other. Think of your discussion as more of a book club than a Bible study.

Reflecting on the Previous Week (30–60 minutes)

From your Personal Bible Experience in Obadiah and Ezekiel this week, have a conversation with your group about what you read by answering the following questions.

What was new or compelling to you?

What questions did you have?

Was there anything that bothered you?

What did you learn about loving God?

What did you learn about loving others?

Preparing for the Week Ahead (15–20 minutes)

WATCH VIDEO WEEK 7: EZEKIEL 25–48

To get the most out of what you will be reading in the coming week, close your time together by watching the video of Bible teacher John Walton explaining the theme, aftermath, and relevance of the last half of Ezekiel. Use the following outline to jot down any additional insights or questions.

VIDEO NOTES

Ezekiel 25–48

Theme of Ezekiel

God as Israel's shepherd (Ezekiel 34)

Overview of Ezekiel 25–48

Oracles against the nations such as Egypt and Tyre (Ezekiel 25–32)

Oracles of restoration after Jerusalem's fall (Ezekiel 33–37)

Elaborated vision: Valley of Dry Bones (Ezekiel 37)

Victory over invaders from the north (Ezekiel 38–39)

Vision of the new Jerusalem and temple (Ezekiel 40–48)

Aftermath of Ezekiel

Regathering of God's people

Return of God's presence

New Covenant and the restoration of David's line

All of the covenant lines are brought back together.

Relevance of Ezekiel

God's ultimate plans and purposes are for his presence to reside among his people.

We partner with God's plan; we don't ask him to join our plans.

THIS WEEK

Read the last half of Ezekiel in *The Books of the Bible, The Prophets*. Maintain your momentum by keeping these guidelines in mind:

- Read what you can.
- Read something every day.
- Always have your *Books of the Bible* with you.
- Every week is a new week.
- Use this study journal as you do your reading for Week 7: Ezekiel, recording any thoughts on the Daily Reading Journal pages.

WEEK 7
EZEKIEL

PERSONAL BIBLE EXPERIENCE

Your personal Bible experience starts with a daily practice of reading the Bible. This week before your group meeting, read the last half of Ezekiel. Use the journaling space to capture your thoughts, questions, responses, emotions, and insights as you read the daily selection. Keep in mind the questions you will be talking about with your discussion group:

- What was new or compelling to you?
- What questions did you have?
- Was there anything that bothered you?
- What did you learn about loving God?
- What did you learn about loving others?

Daily Reading Journal

Day 31: Ezekiel 25:1–28:26 (pages 403–411)

Day 32: Ezekiel 29:1–32:32 (pages 411–419)

Day 33: Ezekiel 33:1–37:28 (pages 419–427)

_____

_____

_____

_____

_____

Day 34: Ezekiel 38:1–43:27 (pages 427–436)

_____

_____

_____

_____

_____

Day 35: Ezekiel 44:1–48:35 (pages 436–444)

_____

_____

_____

_____

_____

 **COMMUNITY BIBLE EXPERIENCE**

Welcome to Session 7 of the Community Bible Experience. You have been experiencing the Bible personally by reading through the last half of the book of Ezekiel this week, and now your group has gathered to experience the Bible in community with each other. Think of your discussion as more of a book club than a Bible study.

Reflecting on the Previous Week (30–60 minutes)

From your Personal Bible Experience in Ezekiel this week, have a conversation with your group about what you read by answering the following questions.

What was new or compelling to you?

What questions did you have?

Was there anything that bothered you?

What did you learn about loving God?

What did you learn about loving others?

Preparing for the Week Ahead (15–20 minutes)

WATCH VIDEO WEEK 8: HAGGAI, ZECHARIAH, JOEL, MALACHI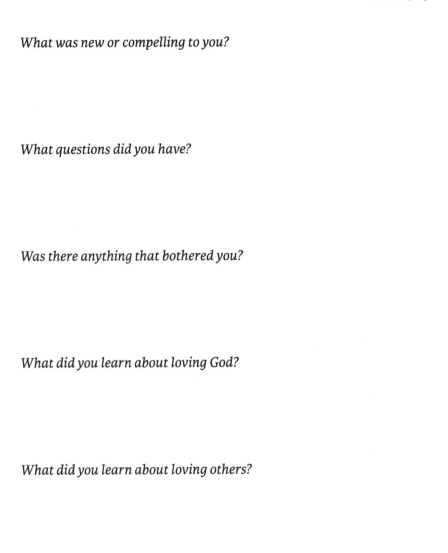

To get the most out of what you will be reading in the coming week, close your time together by watching the video of Bible teacher John Walton explaining the indictment, judgment, instruction, aftermath, and relevance of the books of Haggai, Zechariah, Joel, and Malachi. Use the following outline to jot down any additional insights or questions.

VIDEO NOTES

Post-Exilic Prophets: Prophets after the exile (versus before the exile)

Identity crisis: Are we still God's people? Is he still going to work through us?

Haggai (Persian period, 520 BC)

Three Major Messages

Message 1: "Now or Never" (Haggai 1:1–15). Adjust your priorities; rebuild the temple.

Message 2: "Take Heart, Work" (Haggai 2:1–9). Adjust your perspective; it is God's temple.

Message 3: "Promise and Projection" (Haggai 2:10–23). Adjust your pride; focus on restoration.

Indictment: Self-centeredness and pride

Judgment: Bad harvests are already being experienced.

Instruction: Adjust priorities and perspectives; build the temple.

Aftermath: Bumper crops; Zerubbabel as the sign of the Davidic line

Relevance: Our priorities and perspectives are not always the same as God's.

Zechariah (contemporary of Haggai, Persian empire, October 520 BC–December 518 BC)

Style: Apocalyptic literature, using visions, symbols; visions contain the message, they are not the message.

Problem: What is God doing? It is not our land. God's not here. Who are we?

Indictment: Covenant violations

Judgment: Enemies will attack Jerusalem, yet God will deliver.

Instruction: Repent, return, and establish justice; build the temple.

Aftermath: Restoration, prosperity, deliverance, and kingship

Relevance: God wants to reside in the midst of his people; history is under God's control despite current troubles.

Joel (date uncertain, post-exilic period, after temple built)

Indictment: None

Judgment: Current locust plague, seen as the Day of the Lord

Instruction: Repentance and spiritual renewal

Aftermath: People respond favorably; renewed prosperity; Spirit poured out; deliverance

Relevance: Call on the name of the Lord to be saved.

Malachi (last of the prophets, early 5th century BC; after Haggai, Zechariah, and Joel)

Style: Rhetorical questions

Themes of Malachi

Sin of the priesthood (Malachi 1:6–2:9)

Family offense (Malachi 2:10–16)

Coming of justice (Malachi 2:17–3:5)

Robbing God (Malachi 3:8–12)

God's judgment (Malachi 3:13–4:3)

Indictment: Improper sacrifices and marriage practices; robbing God

Judgment: Purifying

Instruction: Offer appropriate sacrifice; honor marriage; bring the tithe.

Aftermath: Elijah (John the Baptist)

Relevance: God continues to want to be treated as holy so his people reflect their identity as his holy people.

THIS WEEK

Read the books of Haggai, Zechariah, Joel, and Malachi in *The Books of the Bible, The Prophets*. Maintain your momentum by keeping these guidelines in mind:

- Read what you can.
- Read something every day.
- Always have your *Books of the Bible* with you.
- Every week is a new week.
- Use this study journal as you do your reading for Week 8: Haggai, Zechariah, Joel, Malachi, recording any thoughts on the Daily Reading Journal page.

WEEK 8

HAGGAI, ZECHARIAH, JOEL, MALACHI

HAGGAI

The Jews have been released from their Babylonian exile, and they are back in the land. But their work on rebuilding the temple languishes while they work on beautifying their own houses. Haggai preaches a series of sermons to show them that their economic depression is happening because of their indifference to God. Despite their discouragement as they compare this small temple to the former glorious one, he exhorts them to obey God and experience his blessings both now and in the future.

What to watch for in Haggai: Haggai's message to the people is that they can't expect God's blessing if they don't have God's priorities.

ZECHARIAH

Speaking at the same time and for the same reason as Haggai, Zechariah uses symbolic visions, messages, and prophecies to convey his message. Rather than using strong words of rebuke as Haggai did, Zechariah is more of an encourager, inspiring the temple builders to action with the hope of a great outcome for their labors.

What to watch for in Zechariah: Zechariah is another prophet from a priestly lineage (like Jeremiah and Ezekiel), so we see his concern for temple practices in his book. Think about what Zechariah says in regard to the nature of true fasting and its connection to practicing true justice.

JOEL

While other prophets have had to manufacture their object lessons, Joel has his object lesson delivered to his doorstep in the form of a catastrophic locust plague. He seizes the occasion to proclaim God's message that because of Israel's sin, there is a far more devastating judgment to come.

What to watch for in Joel: The book of Joel contains some striking descriptions of the blessing that happens when God's people respond to him with heartfelt contrition.

MALACHI

A century after Haggai and Zechariah exhorted the people to rebuild the temple, the temple worship and general behavior of the people and even the priests had degraded to a level of apathy and corruption that inspired Malachi to speak up. He uses a question-and-answer method to probe their problems of hypocrisy, infidelity, mixed marriages, divorce, false worship, and arrogance. It's rather telling that their non-response to Malachi gets a non-response from God—he is silent for the next 400 years.

What to watch for in Malachi: God tries to get a rise out of his hearers by proposing a test, the only time in Scripture he invites us to test him (page 484). Think about that in light of the general indifference Malachi is trying so hard to dislodge.

 **PERSONAL BIBLE EXPERIENCE**

Your personal Bible experience starts with a daily practice of reading the Bible. This week before your group meeting, read the books of Haggai, Zechariah, Joel, and Malachi. Use the journaling space to capture your thoughts, questions, responses, emotions, and insights as you read the daily selection. Keep in mind the questions you will be talking about with your discussion group:

- What was new or compelling to you?
- What questions did you have?
- Was there anything that bothered you?
- What did you learn about loving God?
- What did you learn about loving others?

Daily Reading Journal

Day 36: Haggai Invitation–Zechariah 8:23 (pages 445–459)

_____

_____

_____

_____

_____

Day 37: Zechariah 9:1–14:21 (pages 459–466)

_____

_____

_____

_____

_____

Day 38: Joel Invitation–3:21 (pages 467–477)

_____

_____

_____

_____

_____

Day 39: Malachi Invitation–4:6 (pages 479–484)

_____

_____

_____

_____

_____

Day 40: GRACE DAY

 **COMMUNITY BIBLE EXPERIENCE**

Welcome to Session 8 of the Community Bible Experience. You have been experiencing the Bible personally by reading through the books of Haggai, Zechariah, Joel, and Malachi this week, and now your group has gathered to experience the Bible in community with each other. Think of your discussion as more of a book club than a Bible study.

Reflecting on the Previous Week (30–60 minutes)

From your Personal Bible Experience in Haggai, Zechariah, Joel, and Malachi this week, have a conversation with your group about what you read by answering the following questions.

What was new or compelling to you?

What questions did you have?

Was there anything that bothered you?

What did you learn about loving God?

What did you learn about loving others?

Final Reflections (15–30 minutes)

Reflect: Give each person a chance to share how their journey through the Prophets impacted them, how it shaped their understanding of the Bible, and what implications it might have for their life.

Rejoice: Celebrate your achievement together! Reading through *The Books of the Bible, The Prophets* in just eight weeks is a major accomplishment.

Regroup: Plan your next meeting.

If you are taking a break before you start the next volume of *The Books of the Bible*, choose the date for your introductory session. To whet your appetite for what's next, read the Invitation to the Writings on page 131 of this journal.

If you are continuing to *The Books of the Bible, The Writings* next week, go ahead and watch the video of Bible teacher John Walton explaining the purpose and relevance of Psalms 1–63, and take notes on pages 134–136 of this journal.

Israel's ancient songs of

PRAISE, LAMENT AND WONDER,

wise words to craft

A GOOD LIFE

and ponder

LIFE'S DEEPEST CHALLENGES,

stories of Israel's

TEMPLE AND WORSHIP,

the birth of a

FESTIVAL,

and visions of

GOD'S COMING RULE

OVER THE WORLD.

THE WRITINGS

INVITATION TO
THE WRITINGS

The Writings are the third major division of the First Testament. They represent a much looser grouping than those in the first and second divisions. They've been drawn together from a wider range of traditions, genres, and time periods. They're presented in this volume grouped by genre, so each work can be read meaningfully alongside other examples of the same kind of literature:

Collections of song lyrics: Psalms, Lamentations, Song of Songs
Wisdom Literature: Proverbs, Ecclesiastes, Job
Temple History: Chronicles-Ezra-Nehemiah, Esther
Historical/Apocalyptic: Daniel

This group of books thus completes the First Testament by drawing a diverse collection of books into its pages. They review the history of the covenant people and display the theological and literary riches they possessed. As one of the psalmists wrote, *God has revealed his word to Jacob, his laws and decrees to Israel.*

INTRODUCTORY SESSION

The Introductory Session introduces your group to *The Books of the Bible, The Writings*. Hold the Introductory Session the week before your first meeting. If you are reading straight through all four volumes, you will only hold one Introductory Session, which will take place before you begin your first volume. If you are spreading out your reading of the four volumes, it is helpful to have an introductory gathering the week before you start each one.

Getting to Know You (15–30 minutes)

If your group is new to each other, or if you have any new members in your group for this session, invite each group member to introduce themselves, using any or all of the following prompts:

- List three of your roles in life and what you like about them.
- What one word describes your past experience of reading the Bible?
- What do you hope to get from this journey of reading *The Books of the Bible, The Writings* together?

Introduction (15–30 minutes)

INTRODUCE THE
COMMUNITY BIBLE EXPERIENCE

Explain how the Community Bible Experience works by summarizing the information in the book introduction, starting on page 7 of this study journal. The key points are:

- Five tips for Bible reading
- Weekly reading plan
- Weekly discussion questions for groups
- Three tips for weekly gatherings

Allow time for discussion about how your group wants to function with each other and to address any concerns people have about doing the Bible reading.

INTRODUCE *THE WRITINGS*

The Books of the Bible, The Writings contains six sections of important introductory material. If time allows, read through all six sections of the introductory material together. If your group has read other volumes in the past, or if you have time constraints, focus on the Drama of the Bible in Six Acts, page iii (it's helpful to read that together before every new series), and read the Invitation to the Writings, page xiv.

Preparing for the Week Ahead (15–20 minutes)

Discuss the challenge of reading 12 pages a day. Remind participants that most readings take around 30 minutes to complete—about the same time it takes to watch a short TV show.

WATCH VIDEO WEEK 1: PSALMS

To get the most out of what you will be reading in the coming week, close your time together by watching the video of Bible teacher John Walton explaining the purpose and relevance of Psalms 1–63. Use the following outline to jot down any additional insights or questions.

VIDEO NOTES

Psalms 1–63

Setting of Psalms: varied; final compilation of Psalms was post-exile

Purpose of Psalms

God's kingship

Psalms does not command prayer, instruct in prayer, or
provide model prayers. Psalms commends prayer, describes
prayers, and illustrates prayer in action.

Authorship of Psalms: Psalm titles mention various authors.

Composition of Psalms

Five books, smaller collections (like the Davidic Group I,
Psalms 3–41)

Purpose of each book is given in the seam psalms

Psalms 1 and 2 introduce the five books

Categories of Psalms

Three major categories: Lament, praise, and wisdom

Similar psalm literature is found in other cultures

Differences concern how they think about God, expectations
of God, and trust in God.

Themes of Psalms, Book 1 (David)

Kingship (Psalms 45, 72, 89, 110, 132, 144) about a future, ideal, Davidic king

Messianic psalms are fulfilled in Jesus (Psalm 22)

God's glory in creation (Psalm 19)

Psalm 8—What is man?

Psalm 23—My shepherd

Psalm 24—King of Glory

Psalm 27—Light and Salvation

Psalm 37—Desires of your heart

Psalm 46—Refuge and strength

Psalm 48—Walk about the towers of Zion, the city of our God

Psalm 51—Create in me a clean heart (a repentance psalm)

Psalm 59—Cursing enemies

Relevance of Psalms, Book 1

How does God's kingship play out in the world?

How does God's kingship play out in our times of trouble?

They show that God is willing to hear our prayers.

THIS WEEK
· · · · · · · · · ·

Read the Psalms 1–62 in *The Books of the Bible, The Writings*. Maintain your momentum by keeping these guidelines in mind:

- Read what you can.
- Read something every day.
- Always have your *Books of the Bible* with you.
- Every week is a new week.
- Use this study journal as you do your reading for Week 1: Psalms, recording any thoughts on the Daily Reading Journal pages.

PSALMS

PSALMS
· · · · · · ·

The book of Psalms, a collection of lyrics for almost 150 worship songs, is the largest and perhaps most widely used book in the Bible. These songs, written over a 700-year period, were collected after the people of Israel returned from exile in Babylon, and became the hymnbook and devotional guide used in the rebuilt temple. The collection is divided into five parts, or "books," reminding the reader of the five books of the law of Moses, and in their general outlines they trace Israel's history in its successive stages:

Book 1 (Psalms 1–41) and Book 2 (Psalms 42–72): Monarchy

The theme of these psalms by David and Korah is God establishing the king on the throne.

Book 3 (Psalms 73–89) and Book 4 (Psalms 90–106): Exile

These psalms by Asaph and anonymous writers lament the destruction of Israel, complain that God has abandoned David's line, plead for the return of the exiled people, yet declare repeatedly that *the* Lord *reigns*—in other words, Israel's true king is still on the throne.

Book 5 (Psalms 107–150): Return

The opening psalm in this section declares that God has brought the exiles back. Many "songs of ascents" are included in this book of psalms by David and anonymous writers—sung by travelers going up to the temple in Jerusalem, suggesting the people have returned to the land.

Each book within Psalms ends with a doxology, and Psalm 150 is the doxology for the entire collection.

What to watch for in Psalms: The central theme of Psalms is worship. Look for what the writers say about God and why he is worthy of our praise.

PERSONAL BIBLE EXPERIENCE

Your personal Bible experience starts with a daily practice of reading the Bible. This week before your group meeting, read the first part of the book of Psalms. Use the journaling space to capture your thoughts, questions, responses, emotions, and insights as you read the daily selection. Keep in mind the questions you will be talking about with your discussion group:

- What was new or compelling to you?
- What questions did you have?
- Was there anything that bothered you?
- What did you learn about loving God?
- What did you learn about loving others?

Daily Reading Journal

Day 1: Psalms Invitation–Psalm 17 (pages 1–16)

_____

_____

_____

_____

_____

Day 2: Psalms 18–29 (pages 17–31)

_____

_____

_____

_____

_____

Day 3: Psalms 30–41 (pages 32–48)

_____

_____

_____

_____

_____

Day 4: Psalms 42–49 (pages 49–57)

_____

_____

_____

_____

Day 5: Psalms 50–62 (pages 58–70)

_____

_____

_____

_____

 **COMMUNITY BIBLE EXPERIENCE**

Welcome to Session 1 of the Community Bible Experience. You have been experiencing the Bible personally by reading the first part of the book of Psalms this week, and now your group has gathered to experience the Bible in community with each other. Think of your discussion as more of a book club than a Bible study.

Reflecting on the Previous Week (30–60 minutes)

From your Personal Bible Experience in the book of Psalms this week, have a conversation with your group about what you read by answering the following questions.

What was new or compelling to you?

What questions did you have?

Was there anything that bothered you?

What did you learn about loving God?

What did you learn about loving others?

Preparing for the Week Ahead (15–20 minutes)

WATCH VIDEO WEEK 2: PSALMS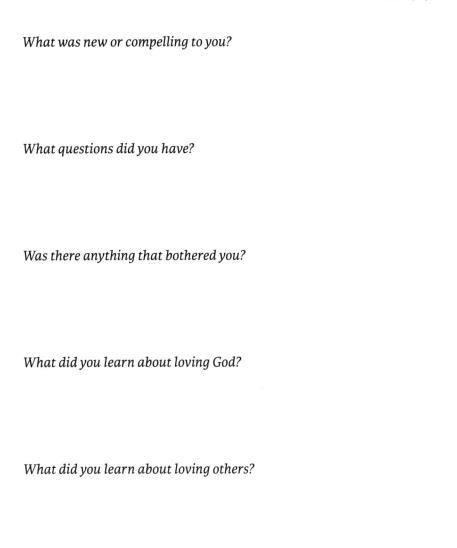

To get the most out of what you will be reading in the coming week, close your time together by watching the video of Bible teacher John Walton explaining the themes and relevance of Psalms 64–119. Use the following outline to jot down any additional insights or questions.

VIDEO NOTES

Themes of Psalms, Book 2 (David)

Lament psalms

The retribution principle: The righteous will prosper and the wicked will suffer (this does not offer guarantees, but tells us about the type of God we serve).

Shame

Deliverance

Vindication

Psalm 72—Kingship

Themes of Psalms, Book 3 (Asaph and Korah)

Psalm 73—The afterlife

Psalm 84—God's presence

Psalm 88—Despair

Psalm 89—Davidic Covenant (the seam psalm of Book 3)

Themes of Psalms, Book 4 (Reflections on the Exile)

Psalm 106:47—Gathering from among the nations

Psalm 90—Begins with Moses

Psalm 93–99—The Lord reigns

Psalm 110—God's kingship, fulfilled in Jesus

Psalm 104—God orders and sustains the natural world

Psalm 105–106—Israel's history

Relevance of Psalms, Books 2–4

Psalms give us a sense of participation with God; we find our place in his story.

THIS WEEK
· · · · · · · · · ·

Read Psalms 63–118 in *The Books of the Bible, The Writings*. Maintain your momentum by keeping these guidelines in mind:

- Read what you can.
- Read something every day.
- Always have your *Books of the Bible* with you.
- Every week is a new week.
- Use this study journal as you do your reading for Week 2: Psalms, recording any thoughts on the Daily Reading Journal pages.

WEEK 2
PSALMS

PERSONAL BIBLE EXPERIENCE

Your personal Bible experience starts with a daily practice of reading the Bible. This week before your group meeting, read Psalms 64–119. Use the journaling space to capture your thoughts, questions, responses, emotions, and insights as you read the daily selection. Keep in mind the questions you will be talking about with your discussion group:

- What was new or compelling to you?
- What questions did you have?
- Was there anything that bothered you?
- What did you learn about loving God?
- What did you learn about loving others?

Daily Reading Journal

Day 6: Psalms 63–72 (pages 71–85)

_____

_____

_____

_____

_____

Day 7: Psalms 73–81 (pages 85–99)

_____

_____

_____

_____

_____

Day 8: Psalms 82–89 (pages 99–108)

_____

_____

_____

_____

_____

Day 9: Psalms 90–106 (pages 108–130)

_____

_____

_____

_____

_____

Day 10: Psalms 107–118 (pages 130–142)

_____

_____

_____

_____

_____

 **COMMUNITY BIBLE EXPERIENCE**

Welcome to Session 2 of the Community Bible Experience. You have been experiencing the Bible personally by reading through the next portion of the book of Psalms this week, and now your group has gathered to experience the Bible in community with each other. Think of your discussion as more of a book club than a Bible study.

Reflecting on the Previous Week (30–60 minutes)

From your Personal Bible Experience in the book of Psalms this week, have a conversation with your group about what you read by answering the following questions.

What was new or compelling to you?

What questions did you have?

Was there anything that bothered you?

What did you learn about loving God?

What did you learn about loving others?

Preparing for the Week Ahead (15–20 minutes)

WATCH VIDEO WEEK 3: PSALMS, LAMENTATIONS, SONG OF SONGS

To get the most out of what you will be reading in the coming week, close your time together by watching the video of Bible teacher John Walton explaining the themes and relevance of the last part of Psalms and the books of Lamentations and Song of Songs. Use the following outline to jot down any additional insights or questions.

VIDEO NOTES

Themes of Psalms Book 5 (Post-exilic Reflections)

Psalm 107—Thankfulness for being gathered

Psalm 119—Torah is a joy and delight to help them live in the sacred space

Psalms 120–134—Ascent songs

Psalm 136—*Hesed*, acting to fulfill an obligation, steadfast love

Psalm 139—Lament

Psalm 145—Conclusion to Book 5

Psalms 146–150—Finale for entire book of Psalms

Relevance of Psalms, Book 5

God is king (Psalm 145).

Prayer as relationship building

Pray prayers of becoming.

Lamentations

National prayers, composed of complex acrostics

Main point: Jerusalem has fallen; the temple is destroyed; God's presence has been lost.

> Because of the LORD's great love we are not consumed,
>> for his compassions never fail.
> They are new every morning;
>> great is your faithfulness.
>
> (LAMENTATIONS 3:22–23)

Song of Songs

History of interpretation

Allegorical

Reconstructing a narrative

Ideals of marriage

Alternative interpretation: Wisdom teaching related to the power of love and sex (Song of Songs 8:6–7)

Relevance of Song of Songs

Wisdom and the need for discipline with the beautiful gifts of love and sex

THIS WEEK
· · · · · · · · · ·

Read the last part of Psalms and the books of Lamentations and Song of Songs in *The Books of the Bible, The Writings*. Maintain your momentum by keeping these guidelines in mind:

- Read what you can.
- Read something every day.
- Always have your *Books of the Bible* with you.
- Every week is a new week.
- Use this study journal as you do your reading for Week 3: Psalms, Lamentations, Song of Songs, recording any thoughts on the Daily Reading Journal pages.

LAMENTATIONS

This small collection of five songs mourns Babylon's destruction of Jerusalem and the deportation of much of its population. The citizens left behind lived in terrible conditions, and the prophet Jeremiah wrote a five-poem acrostic dirge to express sorrow, shame, and grief about the city's desolation.

What to watch for in Lamentations: Despite the dismal circumstance, there is the one note of hope in the middle of the book, a hope based on the faithfulness of the compassionate God of Israel.

SONG OF SONGS

This anthology of wedding songs tells the story of the courtship of a man and woman, of their marriage and its consummation, and of the beginning of their new life together. The dimensions of a romantic relationship in this book include attraction, desire, companionship, pleasure, union, separation, faithfulness, and praise.

What to watch for in Song of Songs: Because of the famously intimate content of Song of Songs which garners most of the attention of the typical reader, here is something you might miss if you're not looking for it—there are twenty-one species of plants and fifteen species of animals mentioned in this book.

PERSONAL BIBLE EXPERIENCE

Your personal Bible experience starts with a daily practice of reading the Bible. This week before your group meeting, read the rest of Psalms and the books of Lamentations and Song of Songs. Use the journaling space to capture your thoughts, questions, responses, emotions, and insights as you read the daily selection. Keep in mind the questions you will be talking about with your discussion group:

- What was new or compelling to you?
- What questions did you have?
- Was there anything that bothered you?
- What did you learn about loving God?
- What did you learn about loving others?

Daily Reading Journal

Day 11: Psalm 119 (pages 143–152)

_____

_____

_____

_____

_____

Day 12: Psalms 120–138 (pages 152–164)

_____

_____

_____

_____

_____

Day 13: Psalms 139–150 (pages 164–175)

_____

_____

_____

_____

_____

Day 14: Lamentations Invitation–5:22 (pages 177–194)

_____

_____

_____

_____

_____

Day 15: Song of Songs Invitation–8:14 (pages 195–208)

_____

_____

_____

_____

_____

 **COMMUNITY BIBLE EXPERIENCE**

Welcome to Session 3 of the Community Bible Experience. You have been experiencing the Bible personally by reading through the last part of Psalms and the books of Lamentations and Song of Songs this week, and now your group has gathered to experience the Bible in community with each other. Think of your discussion as more of a book club than a Bible study.

Reflecting on the Previous Week (30–60 minutes)

From your Personal Bible Experience in Psalms, Lamentations, and Song of Songs this week, have a conversation with your group about what you read by answering the following questions.

What was new or compelling to you?

What questions did you have?

Was there anything that bothered you?

What did you learn about loving God?

What did you learn about loving others?

Preparing for the Week Ahead (15–20 minutes)

WATCH VIDEO WEEK 4: PROVERBS, ECCLESIASTES

To get the most out of what you will be reading in the coming week, close your time together by watching the video of Bible teacher John Walton explaining the themes and relevance of Proverbs and Ecclesiastes. Use the following outline to jot down any additional insights or questions.

VIDEO NOTES

Proverbs

Theme of Proverbs: Wisdom = Order

Proverbs is meant to be learned with others, not as an independent study.

Proverbial literature includes generalizations, not promises (such as Proverbs 22:6).

Truth is found in the values; there aren't any "guarantees."

Ecclesiastes

Theme of Ecclesiastes: Meaningless, vanity, *hebel. Hebel* is the opposite of self-fulfillment; this world cannot offer fulfillment.

We are to find hope in readjusting our thinking.

Both prosperity and adversity come from the hand of God.

Abandon the quest: Self-fulfillment is not what you are after.

Relevance of Proverbs and Ecclesiastes

Fear Yahweh; recognize his worth.

Abandon the quest; fulfillment is a gift from God.

Pursue a God-centered course in life that reflects Yahweh's order.

THIS WEEK

Read the books of Proverbs and Ecclesiastes in *The Books of the Bible, The Writings*. Maintain your momentum by keeping these guidelines in mind:

- Read what you can.
- Read something every day.
- Always have your *Books of the Bible* with you.
- Every week is a new week.
- Use this study journal as you do your reading for Week 4: Proverbs, Ecclesiastes, recording any thought on the Daily Reading Journal pages.

WEEK 4
PROVERBS, ECCLESIASTES

PROVERBS

Proverbs is the most intensely practical book in the First Testament, and it is one of the few biblical books that clearly spells out its purpose, by saying it is *for gaining wisdom and instruction* (page 211). These two complementary words are both needed in life: *wisdom* means "skill" and *instruction* means "discipline"; it requires discipline to perfect a skill. Proverbs is about the fundamental skill of living right, and to perfect that skill it takes the discipline of putting God first in every area of life.

What to watch for in Proverbs: Choose an area of your life you need to work on, such as self-control, the tongue, friendships, pride, anger, or work, and look for the proverbs that address that issue.

ECCLESIASTES

The key word in Ecclesiastes is *meaningless*, which describes the futile emptiness of trying to be happy apart from God. The Teacher in Ecclesiastes has undertaken a diligent quest for purpose, meaning, and satisfaction, but by trying to find them in power, popularity, prestige, and pleasure, he has come up empty—*meaningless*. This book is provocative and unsettling; the Teacher wants to prod the readers out of their complacent assumptions about life and make them reexamine the course they've chosen.

What to watch for in Ecclesiastes: So, what is the answer to the unanswerable questions of life, the explanation for the unexplainable? Look for what the Teacher says is the answer.

PERSONAL BIBLE EXPERIENCE

Your personal Bible experience starts with a daily practice of reading the Bible. This week before your group meeting, read the books of Proverbs and Ecclesiastes. Use the journaling space to capture your thoughts, questions, responses, emotions, and insights as you read the daily selection. Keep in mind the questions you will be talking about with your discussion group:

- What was new or compelling to you?
- What questions did you have?
- Was there anything that bothered you?
- What did you learn about loving God?
- What did you learn about loving others?

Daily Reading Journal

Day 16: Proverbs Invitation–9:18 (pages 209–225)

_____

_____

_____

_____

_____

_____

Day 17: Proverbs 10:1–15:29 (pages 225–237)

_____

_____

_____

_____

_____

_____

Day 18: Proverbs 15:30–22:16 (pages 237–249)

_____

_____

_____

_____

_____

Day 19: Proverbs 22:17–31:31 (pages 250–268)

_____

_____

_____

_____

_____

Day 20: Ecclesiastes Invitation–12:14 (pages 269–288)

_____

_____

_____

_____

_____

COMMUNITY BIBLE EXPERIENCE

Welcome to Session 4 of the Community Bible Experience. You have been experiencing the Bible personally by reading through the books of Proverbs and Ecclesiastes this week, and now your group has gathered to experience the Bible in community with each other. Think of your discussion as more of a book club than a Bible study.

Reflecting on the Previous Week (30–60 minutes)

From your Personal Bible Experience in Proverbs and Ecclesiastes this week, have a conversation with your group about what you read by answering the following questions.

What was new or compelling to you?

What questions did you have?

Was there anything that bothered you?

What did you learn about loving God?

What did you learn about loving others?

Preparing for the Week Ahead (15–20 minutes)

WATCH VIDEO WEEK 5: JOB

To get the most out of what you will be reading in the coming week, close your time together by watching the video of Bible teacher John Walton explaining the misperceptions and relevance of Job. Use the following outline to jot down any additional insights or questions.

VIDEO NOTES

Job—Wisdom Book

Theme of Job

Innocent sufferer

Misperceptions about Job

Job has trials but is not on trial.

Retribution principle: Wicked suffer and righteous prosper

More about God than about Job; God's policies are in question

More about God's wisdom than his justice

Not how to think about suffering, but how to think about God when you are suffering

More about trusting than about answers

More about what constitutes righteousness than about why we suffer

Relevance of Job

Does our righteousness stand up to the test?

Do not think that there is an explanation for what happens to us.

We cannot "out-God" God.

Trust is the only possible response.

God's wisdom prevails.

THIS WEEK
· · · · · · · · · ·

Read the book of Job in *The Books of the Bible, The Writings*. Maintain your momentum by keeping these guidelines in mind:

- Read what you can.
- Read something every day.
- Always have your *Books of the Bible* with you.
- Every week is a new week.
- Use this study journal as you do your reading for Week 5: Job, recording any thoughts on the Daily Reading Journal pages.

JOB

. . . .

In the books of wisdom literature that we have read so far, Proverbs describes how living right will generally lead to success and well-being. Ecclesiastes then warns that success and well-being are not actually guaranteed to anyone because of the crookedness that has come into our world. The book of Job takes this to an extreme, exploring the situation of a righteous person who not only *isn't* rewarded but who suffers the most dire pain through no fault of his own. The fundamental question of the book is, why do the righteous suffer if God is loving and all-powerful? The main theme of the book is not in the first part of that question, why do good people suffer, even though that is what is usually focused on in discussions about Job. Rather, the main message of Job comes from the second part of the question: God is loving and all-powerful, even when his ways are incomprehensible.

What to watch for in Job: Job is a different man at the end of the book than he is at the beginning of the book. Watch his journey from trusting God to complaining to self-righteousness to repentance to restoration.

PERSONAL BIBLE EXPERIENCE

. . . .

Your personal Bible experience starts with a daily practice of reading the Bible. This week before your group meeting, read the book of Job. Use the journaling space to capture your thoughts, questions, responses, emotions, and insights as you read the daily selection. Keep in mind the questions you will be talking about with your discussion group:

- What was new or compelling to you?
- What questions did you have?
- Was there anything that bothered you?
- What did you learn about loving God?
- What did you learn about loving others?

Daily Reading Journal

Day 21: Job Invitation–8:22 (pages 289–303)

_____

_____

_____

_____

_____

Day 22: Job 9:1–15:35 (pages 304–314)

_____

_____

_____

_____

_____

Day 23: Job 16:1–25:6 (pages 314–328)

_____

_____

_____

_____

_____

Day 24: Job 26:1–31:40 (pages 328–337)

_____

_____

_____

_____

_____

Day 25: Job 32:1–42:17 (pages 337–355)

_____

_____

_____

_____

 **COMMUNITY BIBLE EXPERIENCE**

Welcome to Session 5 of the Community Bible Experience. You have been experiencing the Bible personally by reading through the book of Job this week, and now your group has gathered to experience the Bible in community with each other. Think of your discussion as more of a book club than a Bible study.

Reflecting on the Previous Week (30–60 minutes)

From your Personal Bible Experience in Job this week, have a conversation with your group about what you read by answering the following questions.

What was new or compelling to you?

What questions did you have?

Was there anything that bothered you?

What did you learn about loving God?

What did you learn about loving others?

Preparing for the Week Ahead (15–20 minutes)

WATCH VIDEO WEEK 6:
CHRONICLES-EZRA-NEHEMIAH

To get the most out of what you will be reading in the coming week, close your time together by watching the video of Bible teacher John Walton explaining the contrast between Samuel–Kings and the Chronicler. Use the following outline to jot down any additional insights or questions.

VIDEO NOTES

1 Chronicles (400 BC)

Overview of 1 Chronicles

Reflect back on the monarchy of Israel

Almost 150 years after their return from exile

Covenant identity crisis

Chronicles is reflecting on history from a different perspective than that of Samuel–Kings in the Covenant History.

Covenant History	Chronicles
Overall theme is failure	Overall theme of continuity and transformation
Proclamation of doom	Proclamation of the kingdom
Focus on apostasy	Focus on reformers
Ended in judgment	Ends with hope
Addressed to exiles	Addressed to those returned from exile
Explains why God was punishing	Explains how God was preserving

Purpose of genealogies (1 Chronicles 1–9): to renew their identity as people of God, recognize their legacy, beginning with Adam

Retells David's story, especially in regards to covenant and kingship

Relevance of 1 Chronicles

Who are we?

We need to find our place in the people of God.

Apostles' Creed

THIS WEEK
· · · · · · · · · ·

Read the book of 1 Chronicles from Chronicles-Ezra-Nehemiah in *The Books of the Bible, The Writings*. Maintain your momentum by keeping these guidelines in mind:

- Read what you can.
- Read something every day.
- Always have your *Books of the Bible* with you.
- Every week is a new week.
- Use this study journal as you do your reading for Week 6: Chronicles-Ezra-Nehemiah, recording any thoughts on the Daily Reading Journal pages.

CHRONICLES-EZRA-NEHEMIAH

The four books of 1–2 Chronicles, Ezra, and Nehemiah form one long sprawling history that runs all the way from the beginning of the human race to the return from exile at the end of the First Testament. The central concern and the perspective from which all four parts of this narrative are written is the temple: how God chose Jerusalem as the place where he'd be worshiped, how a temple was built there, how it was destroyed, and how it was rebuilt as a place where people of all nations could come to seek the true God.

1–2 Chronicles: If you feel like you have encountered this content before, you're not imagining things. First Chronicles, like 2 Samuel, is dedicated to the life of David. Second Chronicles focuses on Solomon and the southern kings, seen before in 1–2 Kings. But the lens through which the history is told is completely different. While Samuel–Kings gives a political history of Israel and Judah, Chronicles gives a history of the temple, or a religious history. It is fascinating, given that background, to see what Chronicles adds and what it leaves out. For instance, Chronicles adds the most comprehensive genealogy in the Bible, demonstrating God's keeping of his covenant promises by maintaining the Davidic line. We also read the new accounts of David's extensive preparations for the temple, and Solomon's construction and dedication of the temple. What we don't see in Chronicles is any mention of the kings of Israel in the north, and there is but a brief mention of any kings of Judah who had a part in destroying the temple. Only the kings who were Judah's temple restorers are given any prominence.

Ezra-Nehemiah: At this point, there is a convergence of biblical characters you may have already encountered if you read *The Books of the Prophets*. Ezra picks up where Chronicles leaves off, with King Cyrus of Persia allowing the Jews to return to rebuild the temple. Zerubbabel leads the first group of exiles back to start rebuilding, but they only get as far as the temple foundation when work stalls for fourteen years. Enter Haggai and Zechariah, who get the work back on track and the temple is completed. During the next fifty-eight years, the saga of Esther takes place. Then, Ezra leads a smaller contingent of exiles back to Jerusalem, and he rebuilds the spiritual condition of the people. Thirteen years later, Nehemiah arrives and not only rebuilds the walls around Jerusalem, but he works with Ezra to rebuild the people morally so that the restoration will be complete. Malachi, the last prophet of the First Testament, also ministers during his time to provide additional spiritual direction.

What to watch for in Chronicles-Ezra-Nehemiah: Look at what great lengths God goes to through the whole historical record of the First Testament to establish his temple. Interestingly, right when the second temple is being built, Buddha is in India, Confucius is in China, and Socrates is in Greece, all building their own centers of religion and philosophical thought.

PERSONAL BIBLE EXPERIENCE

Your personal Bible experience starts with a daily practice of reading the Bible. This week before your group meeting, read 1 Chronicles from the book of Chronicles-Ezra-Nehemiah. Use the journaling space to capture your thoughts, questions, responses, emotions, and insights as you read the daily selection. Keep in mind the questions you will be talking about with your discussion group:

- What was new or compelling to you?
- What questions did you have?
- Was there anything that bothered you?
- What did you learn about loving God?
- What did you learn about loving others?

Daily Reading Journal

Day 26: Chronicles-Ezra-Nehemiah Invitation–1 Chronicles 5:26
(pages 357–371)

_____

_____

_____

_____

_____

Day 27: 1 Chronicles 6:1–10:14 (pages 371–382)

_____

_____

_____

_____

_____

Day 28: 1 Chronicles 11:1–17:27 (pages 382–394)

_____

_____

_____

_____

_____

Day 29: 1 Chronicles 18:1–27:34 (pages 394–409)

_____

_____

_____

_____

_____

Day 30: 1 Chronicles 28:1–29:30 (pages 409–412)

_____

_____

_____

_____

_____

 **COMMUNITY BIBLE EXPERIENCE**

Welcome to Session 6 of the Community Bible Experience. You have been experiencing the Bible personally by reading 1 Chronicles from the book of Chronicles-Ezra-Nehemiah, and now your group has gathered to experience the Bible in community with each other. Think of your discussion as more of a book club than a Bible study.

Reflecting on the Previous Week (30–60 minutes)

From your Personal Bible Experience in Chronicles-Ezra-Nehemiah this week, have a conversation with your group about what you read by answering the following questions.

What was new or compelling to you?

What questions did you have?

Was there anything that bothered you?

What did you learn about loving God?

What did you learn about loving others?

Preparing for the Week Ahead (15–20 minutes)

WATCH VIDEO WEEK 7:
CHRONICLES-EZRA-NEHEMIAH
· ·

To get the most out of what you will be reading in the coming week, close your time together by watching the video of Bible teacher John Walton explaining the themes and relevance of 2 Chronicles and Ezra. Use the following outline to jot down any additional insights or questions.

VIDEO NOTES

2 Chronicles

Themes of Chronicles

Levites and temple

God chose them as his people to dwell among them; this was the purpose of the covenant.

Chronicles focuses on God's presence, not political kingdom.

Messianism and the kingdom of God: Think about God's kingship even when there is no king.

Retribution theology: Wicked kings are punished; righteous kings prosper.

Relevance of Chronicles

God's preservation of his people as he continues his plans and purposes

Ezra (458 BC)

Overview of Ezra

Recounts the first return from exile and building the temple

The support of royal decrees indicates God's blessing.

Recounts local opposition

Significance of the return as the fulfillment of God's prophets

Goal of Ezra: to restore the Torah as the basis for community in the presence of a holy God

Themes of Ezra

Role of the Persian kings

Separation of the community for purposes of identity

Relevance of Ezra

Importance of God's people recognizing their identity and living
into it

God works out his plans and purposes against all odds.

THIS WEEK

Read 2 Chronicles and Ezra from the book of Chronicles-Ezra-Nehemiah
in *The Books of the Bible, The Writings*. Maintain your momentum by
keeping these guidelines in mind:

- Read what you can.
- Read something every day.
- Always have your *Books of the Bible* with you.
- Every week is a new week.
- Use this study journal as you do your reading for Week 7:
  Chronicles-Ezra-Nehemiah, recording any thoughts on the Daily
  Reading Journal pages.

WEEK 7
CHRONICLES-EZRA-NEHEMIAH

PERSONAL BIBLE EXPERIENCE

Your personal Bible experience starts with a daily practice of reading the Bible. This week before your group meeting, read 2 Chronicles and Ezra from the book of Chronicles-Ezra-Nehemiah. Use the journaling space to capture your thoughts, questions, responses, emotions, and insights as you read the daily selection. Keep in mind the questions you will be talking about with your discussion group:

- What was new or compelling to you?
- What questions did you have?
- Was there anything that bothered you?
- What did you learn about loving God?
- What did you learn about loving others?

Daily Reading Journal

Day 31: 2 Chronicles 1:1–14:1 (pages 412–429)

_____

_____

_____

_____

_____

_____

Day 32: 2 Chronicles 14:2–21:20 (pages 429–439)

_____

_____

_____

_____

_____

_____

Day 33: 2 Chronicles 22:1–28:27 (pages 439–448)

_____

_____

_____

_____

_____

_____

Day 34: 2 Chronicles 29:1–36:21 (pages 448–463)

_____

_____

_____

_____

_____

Day 35: 2 Chronicles 36:22–Ezra 10:44 (pages 463–480)

_____

_____

_____

_____

_____

 **COMMUNITY BIBLE EXPERIENCE**

Welcome to Session 7 of the Community Bible Experience. You have been experiencing the Bible personally by reading 2 Chronicles and Ezra from the book of Chronicles-Ezra-Nehemiah this week, and now your group has gathered to experience the Bible in community with each other. Think of your discussion as more of a book club than a Bible study.

Reflecting on the Previous Week (30–60 minutes)

From your Personal Bible Experience in Chronicles-Ezra-Nehemiah this week, have a conversation with your group about what you read by answering the following questions.

What was new or compelling to you?

What questions did you have?

Was there anything that bothered you?

What did you learn about loving God?

What did you learn about loving others?

Preparing for the Week Ahead (15–20 minutes)

WATCH VIDEO WEEK 8: ESTHER, DANIEL

To get the most out of what you will be reading in the coming week, close your time together by watching the video of Bible teacher John Walton explaining the indictment, judgment, instruction, aftermath, and relevance of the books of Nehemiah, Esther, and Daniel. Use the following outline to jot down any additional insights or questions.

VIDEO NOTES

Nehemiah (originally combined with Ezra)

Nehemiah hears about Jerusalem and asks Persian king Artaxerxes to rebuild Jerusalem's walls.

Themes of Nehemiah

Prayer and trust

Rebuilding Jerusalem despite opposition

Reading of the Torah is accompanied by confession.

Relevance of Nehemiah

God's preservation of his people as he continues his plans and
purposes

What Nehemiah is *not*: a leadership model or a source of
regulations for divorce and remarriage

God continues to carry out plans and purposes through people,
against all odds.

Esther (a generation earlier than Ezra-Nehemiah, during Persian King Xerxes)

Literary craft: Use of irony and hidden information

Yahweh is never mentioned

Theme of Esther

Yahweh is at work behind the scenes

Relevance of Esther

God preserves his people.

God works through unlikely people.

God judges those who stand against him.

There is always more going on than meets the eye.

Daniel (600–200 BC, from Neo-Babylonian period through Persian and Hellenistic periods, up to Maccabees)

Themes of Daniel

Sovereignty of God

Earthly kingdoms are temporary; the everlasting kingdom of God is coming.

Live a life of faith in a hostile world, even while God's restoration is long in coming.

Relevance of Daniel

God's preservation of faithful people

God carries out his plans and purposes both through and despite major empires.

Conclusion of the First Testament: God's Story

God created us to be in relationship with us and to dwell among us.

THIS WEEK
· · · · · · · · · ·

Read Nehemiah from the book of Chronicles-Ezra-Nehemiah and Esther and Daniel in *The Books of the Bible, The Writings*. Maintain your momentum by keeping these guidelines in mind:

- Read what you can.
- Read something every day.
- Always have your *Books of the Bible* with you.
- Every week is a new week.
- Use this study journal as you do your reading for Week 8: Esther, Daniel, recording any thoughts on the Daily Reading Journal pages.

WEEK 8

ESTHER, DANIEL

ESTHER

The story of Esther documents why the festival of Purim has a legitimate place in the cycle of annual festivals established originally by the law of Moses. As in the other book of temple history, Chronicles-Ezra-Nehemiah, which shows holidays such as Passover and the Feast of the Tabernacles having their origin in God's mighty acts of deliverance, Purim too commemorates God's deliverance: when he intervened to save all the Jews who remained in Persia after the first exiles had returned to Palestine.

What to watch for in Esther: Although God's name is not mentioned in this book, God's hand is evident throughout. Look for the coincidences, placements, provisions, and protection of God in this story.

DANIEL

The book of Daniel covers the entire seventy-year period of the Babylonian captivity, and has two distinct halves. The first half presents six stories of how God preserved, protected and promoted four Judeans who were exiled to Babylon as young men. The second half employs Daniel's spiritual gift of interpreting dreams and, in the same apocalyptic style as the book of Revelation, describes four communications he received from God in the later years of his life. Of particular note is his vision of the sixty-nine weeks, which pinpoints the triumphal entry of the Messiah 483 years later, on March 29, AD 33.

What to watch for in Daniel: Daniel is one of the few well-known Bible characters about whom nothing negative is ever written. His life was characterized by faith, prayer, courage, and lack of compromise.

PERSONAL BIBLE EXPERIENCE

Your personal Bible experience starts with a daily practice of reading the Bible. This week before your group meeting, read Nehemiah from the book of Chronicles-Ezra-Nehemiah, and Esther and Daniel. Use the journaling space to capture your thoughts, questions, responses, emotions, and insights as you read the daily selection. Keep in mind the questions you will be talking about with your discussion group:

- What was new or compelling to you?
- What questions did you have?
- Was there anything that bothered you?
- What did you learn about loving God?
- What did you learn about loving others?

Daily Reading Journal

Day 36: Nehemiah 1:1–7:73a (pages 480–490)

_____

_____

_____

_____

_____

_____

Day 37: Nehemiah 7:73b–13:31 (pages 490–502)

_____

_____

_____

_____

_____

_____

Day 38: Esther Invitation–10:3 (pages 503–515)

_____

_____

_____

_____

_____

Day 39: Daniel Invitation–6:28 (pages 517–531)

_____

_____

_____

_____

_____

Day 40: Daniel 7:1–12:13 (pages 531–541)

_____

_____

_____

_____

_____

COMMUNITY BIBLE EXPERIENCE

Welcome to Session 8 of the Community Bible Experience. You have been experiencing the Bible personally by reading Nehemiah from the book of Chronicles-Ezra-Nehemiah, and Esther and Daniel this week, and now your group has gathered to experience the Bible in community with each other. Think of your discussion as more of a book club than a Bible study.

Reflecting on the Previous Week (30–60 minutes)

From your Personal Bible Experience in Chronicles-Ezra-Nehemiah, Esther, and Daniel this week, have a conversation with your group about what you read by answering the following questions.

What was new or compelling to you?

What questions did you have?

Was there anything that bothered you?

What did you learn about loving God?

What did you learn about loving others?

Final Reflections (15–30 minutes)

Reflect: Give each person a chance to share how their journey through the Writings impacted them, how it shaped their understanding of the Bible, and what implications it might have for their life.

Rejoice: Celebrate your achievement together! Reading through *The Books of the Bible, The Writings* in just eight weeks is a major accomplishment. For groups that started with *The Books of the Bible, New Testament*, this is the end of your journey through the entire Bible. If you have read all four volumes of *The Books of the Bible*, rejoice all the more! You have achieved a milestone that for some of you, you may have never thought possible. Take some time to thank one another for providing the community support and encouragement it took to finish this journey together.

Regroup: Plan your next meeting.

If you are taking a break before you start the next volume of *The Books of the Bible*, choose the date for your introductory session. To whet your appetite for what's next, read the Invitation to the New Testament on page 189 of this journal.

If you are continuing to *The Books of the Bible, New Testament* next week, go ahead and watch the video of Bible teacher Jeff Manion explaining the themes and relevance of Luke, and take notes on pages 192–194 of this journal.

Israel's continuing story and its climax in

THE LIFE, DEATH,

AND RESURRECTION OF

JESUS THE MESSIAH,

the announcement of

GOD'S VICTORY OVER HUMANITY'S

ENEMIES SIN AND DEATH,

and the invitation for

ALL PEOPLES TO BE

RECONCILED TO GOD

and to share in his

RESTORATION OF ALL THINGS.

THE NEW TESTAMENT

INVITATION TO
New Testament

The New Testament is the second of the two major divisions in the Bible, filling the final one-quarter of its pages. It continues the story, begun in the First Testament, of how God is restoring his original purpose in creation by working through the chosen people of Israel. It tells specifically how this story reached its crowning moment in the first century AD as Jesus of Nazareth, Israel's Messiah, answered the question of who God is and what he's like once and for all. Through his teaching, Jesus revealed the deepest meaning of the laws and institutions God gave to the people of Israel. Through his death and resurrection, Jesus introduced the forgiveness and life of the age to come into the present age. The New Testament also tells how the followers of Jesus formed a new community and invited people from all over the world to join them. It describes how they worked together to live out the reign of God that Jesus had announced and begun. Finally, the New Testament looks ahead to the day when Jesus will return to renew all of creation and to establish God's justice and peace throughout the earth.

Introductory Session

The Introductory Session introduces your group to *The Books of the Bible, New Testament*. Hold the Introductory Session the week before your first meeting. If you are reading straight through all four volumes, you will only hold one Introductory Session, which will take place before you begin your first volume. If you are spreading out your reading of the four volumes, it is helpful to have an introductory gathering the week before you start each one.

Getting to Know You (15–30 minutes)

If your group is new to each other, or if you have any new members in your group for this session, invite each group member to introduce themselves, using any or all of the following prompts:

- List three of your roles in life and what you like about them.
- What one word describes your past experience of reading the Bible?
- What do you hope to get from this journey of reading *The Books of the Bible, New Testament* together?

Introduction (15–30 minutes)

INTRODUCE THE
COMMUNITY BIBLE EXPERIENCE

Explain how the Community Bible Experience works by summarizing the information in the book introduction, starting on page 7 of this study journal. The key points are:

- Five tips for Bible reading
- Weekly reading plan
- Weekly discussion questions for groups
- Three tips for weekly gatherings

Allow time for discussion about how your group wants to function with each other and to address any concerns people have about doing the Bible reading.

INTRODUCE THE *NEW TESTAMENT*

The Books of the Bible, New Testament contains six sections of important introductory material. If time allows, read through all six sections of the introductory material together. If your group has read other volumes in the past, or if you have time constraints, focus on the Drama of the Bible in Six Acts, page iii (it's helpful to read that together before every new series), and read the Invitation to the New Testament, page xv.

Preparing for the Week Ahead (15–20 minutes)

Discuss the challenge of reading 12 pages a day. Remind participants that most readings take around 30 minutes to complete—about the same time it takes to watch a short TV show.

WATCH VIDEO WEEK 1: LUKE–ACTS

To get the most out of what you will be reading in the coming week, close your time together by watching the video of Bible teacher Jeff Manion introducing the New Testament and explaining the themes and relevance of Luke. Use the following outline to jot down any additional insights or questions.

VIDEO NOTES

What Is the New Testament?

The Old Testament asks, how can the presence of God be restored?

In the New Testament, there is something new: God himself enters the planet in Jesus.

New Testament has twenty-seven books:

Gospels (4 books)

The book of Acts

Epistles (21 books)

The book of Revelation

As you read, keep the first-century audience in mind: "What did it mean to them?" Then, "What does it mean to me?"

New Testament was written by nine human authors and the Divine Author.

Luke

Gospel means "good news"

Themes of Luke

Early events of Jesus's life

Women: First-century world was very patriarchal

Meals

Holy Spirit

Relevance of Luke

How might God be calling your voice?

THIS WEEK
· · · · · · · · · ·

Read the book of Luke–Acts in *The Books of the Bible, New Testament.*
Maintain your momentum by keeping these guidelines in mind:

- Read what you can.
- Read something every day.
- Always have your *Books of the Bible* with you.
- Every week is a new week.
- Use this study journal as you do your reading for Week 1: Luke–
  Acts, recording any thoughts on the Daily Reading Journal pages.

WEEK 1
LUKE–ACTS

LUKE
· · · · ·

We have reunited the two volumes of Luke–Acts and placed them first because they provide an overview of the New Testament period. Luke wrote this two-volume history to serve several important purposes:

1. He wanted to assure followers of Jesus that what they'd been taught about him was trustworthy.
2. Luke documents how God kept the promise he made to the people of Israel by sending them their long-awaited Messiah, demonstrating that the true God is faithful and can be trusted completely.
3. He proves that the extension of God's blessings to the Gentiles is not a fickle change of plans but rather the masterful fulfillment of a plan God has been pursuing over the ages.

What to watch for in Luke: Keep watch for some unlikely cast members in Luke's drama. Luke highlights Jesus's compassion toward the outsiders and outcasts of his day: the poor, the disabled, tax collectors, women, children, and others. According to Luke, Jesus is for everybody.

 **PERSONAL BIBLE EXPERIENCE**
· ·

Your personal Bible experience starts with a daily practice of reading the Bible. This week before your group meeting, read the book of Luke. Use the journaling space to capture your thoughts, questions, responses, emotions, and insights as you read the daily selection. Keep in mind the questions you will be talking about with your discussion group:

- What was new or compelling to you?
- What questions did you have?
- Was there anything that bothered you?
- What did you learn about loving God?
- What did you learn about loving others?

Daily Reading Journal

Day 1: Luke–Acts Invitation–Luke 4:13 (pages 1–11)

_____

_____

_____

_____

_____

Day 2: Luke 4:14–9:50 (pages 11–24)

_____

_____

_____

_____

_____

Day 3: Luke 9:51–13:21 (pages 25–33)

_____

_____

_____

_____

_____

Day 4: Luke 13:22–19:27 (pages 33–42)

_____

_____

_____

_____

_____

Day 5: Luke 19:28–24:53 (pages 42–54)

_____

_____

_____

_____

_____

 **COMMUNITY BIBLE EXPERIENCE**

Welcome to Session 2 of the Community Bible Experience. You have been experiencing the Bible personally by reading through the book of Luke this week, and now your group has gathered to experience the Bible in community with each other. Think of your discussion as more of a book club than a Bible study.

Reflecting on the Previous Week (30–60 minutes)

From your Personal Bible Experience in Luke this week, have a conversation with your group about what you read by answering the following questions.

What was new or compelling to you?

What questions did you have?

Was there anything that bothered you?

What did you learn about loving God?

What did you learn about loving others?

Preparing for the Week Ahead (15–20 minutes)

WATCH VIDEO WEEK 2:
LUKE–ACTS, 1–2 THESSALONIANS

To get the most out of what you will be reading in the coming week, close your time together by watching the video of Bible teacher Jeff Manion explaining the themes and relevance of Acts and 1–2 Thessalonians. Use the following outline to jot down any additional insights or questions.

VIDEO NOTES

Acts

What the disciples did after Jesus ascended

Key to Acts: Movement

> But you will receive power when the Holy Spirit comes on you; and you will be my witnesses in Jerusalem, and in all Judea and Samaria, and to the ends of the earth.
>
> (ACTS 1:8)

Key Event: At Pentecost, the Spirit descends

Key Picture of Transformation: Community

Key Lesson: God is at work in our disappointment

Key Figure: Saul

> [Saul] fell to the ground and heard a voice say to him, "Saul,
> Saul, why do you persecute me?" "Who are you, Lord?" Saul
> asked. "I am Jesus, whom you are persecuting," he replied.
>
> (ACTS 9:4–5)

Key City: Antioch

Themes of Acts

Places

Sermons

Conflict and persecution

Movement of the Holy Spirit

Relevance of Acts

Jesus wants to be known

1–2 Thessalonians

Purpose of 1–2 Thessalonians

To encourage the Thessalonians in their faith

Themes of 1–2 Thessalonians

Encouragement in their suffering

Make a clean break from their old life, and step into their new life

Comfort

THIS WEEK
· · · · · · · · ·

Read the Acts from the book of Luke–Acts and 1–2 Thessalonians in *The Books of the Bible, New Testament.* Maintain your momentum by keeping these guidelines in mind:

- Read what you can.
- Read something every day.
- Always have your *Books of the Bible* with you.
- Every week is a new week.
- Use this study journal as you do your reading for Week 2: Luke– Acts, 1–2 Thessalonians, recording any thoughts on the Daily Reading Journal pages.

WEEK 2
Luke–Acts, 1–2 Thessalonians

ACTS

While Luke's first volume tracked Jesus as he worked his way toward Jerusalem where he gave his life and then rose again, Luke's second volume, Acts, follows the community of Jesus-followers outward from Jerusalem as they expand and spread the good news to Asia, Europe, and eventually Rome.

What to watch for in Acts: Notice how God uses hardship to advance the good news about Jesus. In Acts, the church's expansion beyond Jerusalem is a direct result of religious persecution that backfires.

1–2 THESSALONIANS

These are among Paul's earliest letters. In his first letter to the new church at Thessalonica (in modern-day Greece), Paul encourages believers to hold on to their faith despite intense opposition. Paul writes his second letter to correct a false report that the "day of the Lord" had come without the vindication the Thessalonians were hoping for.

What to watch for in 1–2 Thessalonians: To better appreciate the context of these letters, think back to Paul's experience in Thessalonica with the jealous Jews who rioted, then followed him to Berea and disrupted his efforts again (page 86). Paul knew the believers in Thessalonica would be facing violent opposition.

PERSONAL BIBLE EXPERIENCE

Your personal Bible experience starts with a daily practice of reading the Bible. This week before your group meeting, read Acts from the book of Luke–Acts, and 1–2 Thessalonians. Use the journaling space to capture your thoughts, questions, responses, emotions, and insights as you read the daily selection. Keep in mind the questions you will be talking about with your discussion group:

- What was new or compelling to you?
- What questions did you have?
- Was there anything that bothered you?
- What did you learn about loving God?
- What did you learn about loving others?

Daily Reading Journal

Day 6: Acts 1:1–6:7 (pages 55–64)

_____

_____

_____

_____

_____

_____

Day 7: Acts 6:8–12:24 (pages 64–75)

_____

_____

_____

_____

_____

_____

Day 8: Acts 12:25–19:20 (pages 75–86)

_____

_____

_____

_____

_____

_____

Day 9: Acts 19:21–28:31 (pages 87–102)

_____

_____

_____

_____

_____

_____

Day 10: 1 Thessalonians Invitation–2 Thessalonians 3:18 (pages
103–115)

_____

_____

_____

_____

_____

_____

 **COMMUNITY BIBLE EXPERIENCE**

Welcome to Session 2 of the Community Bible Experience. You have
been experiencing the Bible personally by reading through Acts in the
book of Luke–Acts and 1–2 Thessalonians this week, and now your
group has gathered to experience the Bible in community with each
other. Think of your discussion as more of a book club than a Bible
study.

Reflecting on the Previous Week (30–60 minutes)

From your Personal Bible Experience in Luke–Acts and 1–2 Thessalonians this week, have a conversation with your group about what you read by answering the following questions.

What was new or compelling to you?

What questions did you have?

Was there anything that bothered you?

What did you learn about loving God?

What did you learn about loving others?

Preparing for the Week Ahead (15–20 minutes)

WATCH VIDEO WEEK 3:
1–2 CORINTHIANS, GALATIANS, ROMANS

To get the most out of what you will be reading in the coming week, close your time together by watching the video of Bible teacher Jeff Manion explaining the topics and relevance of 1–2 Corinthians, Galatians, and Romans. Use the following outline to jot down any additional insights or questions.

VIDEO NOTES

1 Corinthians

Topics in 1 Corinthians

Gave Paul's answers to the Corinthians' questions:

Can a Christian eat food sacrificed to idols? In reply, Paul asked, how does your decision affect other believers? How does it help you love?

Why is there a resurrection of the body?

Gave Paul's response to Corinthians' problems:

Division, factions, believers suing each other

People were not sharing food during the Lord's Supper.

2 Corinthians

Topics in 2 Corinthians

Paul's defense of his reputation

God's comfort in trials

> Praise be to the God and Father of our Lord Jesus Christ,
> the Father of compassion and the God of all comfort, who
> comforts us in all our troubles, so that we can comfort
> those in any trouble with the comfort we ourselves re-
> ceive from God.
>
> (2 CORINTHIANS 1:3–4)

Offerings and generosity

> For you know the grace of our Lord Jesus Christ, that
> though he was rich, yet for your sake he became poor, so
> that you through his poverty might become rich.
>
> (2 CORINTHIANS 8:9)

Galatians

Problem in Galatians

People were from Gentile backgrounds, and Judaizers were
confusing them, saying faith in Jesus was insufficient to save.

Key topic in Galatians

Inner transformation and the fruit of the Spirit

Romans

Topics in Romans

Central point: Gospel (good news)

Bad news: We are born rebellious

Righteousness: What does it mean for a deeply flawed person to be right with God?

Words describing our new relationship with Christ: Justification, redemption, sanctification

Justification: God declaring guilty people just

Redemption: Set free because of Christ

Sanctification: Learning to live the new life

Relevance of Romans

Fresh encounter with God's love, mercy, and grace

THIS WEEK

Read the books of 1–2 Corinthians, Galatians, and half of Romans in *The Books of the Bible, New Testament*. Maintain your momentum by keeping these guidelines in mind:

- Read what you can.
- Read something every day.
- Always have your *Books of the Bible* with you.
- Every week is a new week.
- Use this study journal as you do your reading for Week 3: 1–2 Corinthians, Galatians, Romans, recording any thoughts on the Daily Reading Journal pages.

WEEK 3
1–2 CORINTHIANS, GALATIANS, ROMANS

1 CORINTHIANS

This letter is Paul's response to a letter he received from the church he founded in Corinth. He addresses several questions they asked him, and he also challenges some of their practices.

What to watch for in 1 Corinthians: This letter is not for the faint of heart. At times Paul is intense, angry, even sarcastic. The church in Corinth was on the brink of destroying itself, and he loved them too much to let them stay on their downward slide.

2 CORINTHIANS

Paul experienced a great deal of conflict with the church he started in Corinth. After they reaffirmed their respect for his authority, Paul wrote 2 Corinthians to reassure them as well as to address some new problems.

What to watch for in 2 Corinthians: Watch for the recurring theme of comfort. Paul uses the word 13 times in this letter.

GALATIANS

This letter to Gentile believers in Galatia (modern-day Turkey) refutes the idea that they had to observe Jewish customs in order to be saved.

What to watch for in Galatians: Notice how Paul connects Jesus to the story of Israel, arguing that all who follow Christ are children of Abraham.

ROMANS

Unlike his earlier letters, Paul addresses Romans to a church he hadn't met before. He writes to introduce himself and to argue that God wants to rescue Jews and non-Jews alike through Jesus's death and resurrection.

What to watch for in Romans: Romans is one of the most hotly debated books in the New Testament. Keep in mind that the purpose of all the complex theology is to call Gentiles to "the obedience that comes from faith."

 **PERSONAL BIBLE EXPERIENCE**

Your personal Bible experience starts with a daily practice of reading the Bible. This week before your group meeting, read the books of 1–2 Corinthians, Galatians, and half of Romans. Use the journaling space to capture your thoughts, questions, responses, emotions, and insights as you read the daily selection. Keep in mind the questions you will be talking about with your discussion group:

- What was new or compelling to you?
- What questions did you have?
- Was there anything that bothered you?
- What did you learn about loving God?
- What did you learn about loving others?

Daily Reading Journal

Day 11: 1 Corinthians Invitation–7:40 (pages 117–126)

_____

_____

_____

_____

_____

_____

Day 12: 1 Corinthians 8:1–16:24 (pages 127–138)

_____

_____

_____

_____

_____

_____

Day 13: 2 Corinthians Invitation–13:14 (pages 139–153)

_____

_____

_____

_____

_____

_____

Day 14: Galatians Invitation–6:18 (pages 155–163)

_____

_____

_____

_____

_____

_____

Day 15: Romans Invitation–8:39 (pages 165–177)

_____

_____

_____

_____

_____

_____

 **COMMUNITY BIBLE EXPERIENCE**

Welcome to Session 3 of the Community Bible Experience. You have been experiencing the Bible personally by reading through the books of 1–2 Corinthians, Galatians, and half of Romans this week, and now your group has gathered to experience the Bible in community with each other. Think of your discussion as more of a book club than a Bible study.

Reflecting on the Previous Week (30–60 minutes)

From your Personal Bible Experience in 1–2 Corinthians, Galatians, and Romans this week, have a conversation with your group about what you read by answering the following questions.

What was new or compelling to you?

What questions did you have?

Was there anything that bothered you?

What did you learn about loving God?

What did you learn about loving others?

Preparing for the Week Ahead (15–20 minutes)

WATCH VIDEO WEEK 4: ROMANS, COLOSSIANS, EPHESIANS, PHILEMON, PHILIPPIANS, 1 TIMOTHY, TITUS, 2 TIMOTHY ▶

To get the most out of what you will be reading in the coming week, close your time together by watching the video of Bible teacher Jeff Manion explaining the topics and relevance of the rest of Paul's letters. Use the following outline to jot down any additional insights or questions.

VIDEO NOTES

PRISON EPISTLES

Colossians

Purpose of Colossians: To encourage growing faith, but growing faith is threatened faith

> So then, just as you received Christ Jesus as Lord, continue to live your lives in him, rooted and built up in him, strengthened in the faith as you were taught, and overflowing with thankfulness.
>
> (COLOSSIANS 2:6–7)

Ephesians

First half of Ephesians: Belonging and indicative

Second half of Ephesians: Commands and imperatives

Image of belonging: Adoption

Message of Ephesians: Belonging first, behavior second

Philemon

Paul's plea to Philemon to restore the runaway slave, Onesimus

Philippians

Thanks for the gift and friendship

Problem: Addressed selfishness

Relevance of Philippians

When we are where we don't want to be, God can use our lives
powerfully.

Learn to say, "God, I will trust you in this place."

PASTORAL EPISTLES

1 Timothy

Topics in 1 Timothy

Qualifications for elders

Guidance for rich believers

> But godliness with contentment is great gain. For we brought nothing into the world, and we can take nothing out of it.
>
> (1 TIMOTHY 6:6–7)

> Command those who are rich in this present world not to be arrogant nor to put their hope in wealth, which is so uncertain, but to put their hope in God, who richly provides us with everything for our enjoyment.
>
> (1 TIMOTHY 6:17)

Relevance of 1 Timothy

Guidance for an affluent culture

Titus

Message of Titus

Believers' behavior can influence unbelievers' perception of Jesus

> Teach slaves to be subject to their masters in everything,
> to try to please them, not to talk back to them, and not to
> steal from them, but to show that they can be fully trust-
> ed, so that in every way they will make the teaching about
> God our Savior attractive.
>
> (TITUS 2:9–10)

Relevance of Titus

The way we live reflects on the reputation of Jesus

2 Timothy

Relevance of 2 Timothy

God can transform hearts

THIS WEEK
· · · · · · · · · ·

Read the last part of Romans and the books of Colossians, Ephesians, Philemon, Philippians, 1 Timothy, Titus, and 2 Timothy in *The Books of the Bible, New Testament*. Maintain your momentum by keeping these guidelines in mind:

- Read what you can.
- Read something every day.
- Always have your *Books of the Bible* with you.
- Every week is a new week.
- Use this study journal as you do your reading for Week 4: Romans, Colossians, Ephesians, Philemon, Philippians, 1 Timothy, Titus, 2 Timothy, recording any thoughts on the Daily Reading Journal pages.

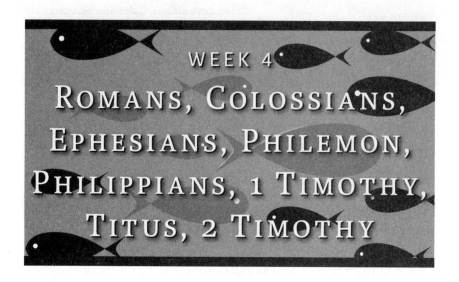

COLOSSIANS

While Paul was sitting in a Roman prison awaiting trial, he penned this letter to the church in Colossae (modern-day Turkey) to warn about those who insisted on religious observances, secret spiritual knowledge, or harsh treatment of the body as necessary for salvation.

What to watch for in Colossians: Notice how Paul alternates between pragmatic exhortation and lyrical prose. It's thought the paragraph starting at the end of page 199 is an early hymn to the supremacy of Christ.

EPHESIANS

This was a general letter circulated among the churches of Asia Minor (modern-day Turkey), encouraging Gentile converts to replace their old way of life with one of purity and integrity.

What to watch for in Ephesians: Look for recurring themes from Paul's other letters, such as the relationship between Jewish and Gentile believers (see Romans) or the supremacy of Christ (see Colossians).

PHILEMON

Philemon was a wealthy man living in Colossae, whose slave, Onesimus, had run away. While on the run, Onesimus had put his faith in Jesus and become Paul's assistant. Paul sent him back to face his former master, this letter in hand, pleading with Philemon to welcome Onesimus "no longer as a slave, but . . . as a dear brother."

What to watch for in Philemon: Notice how Paul employs every ounce of persuasion to prevail upon Philemon.

PHILIPPIANS

The believers in Philippi (modern-day Greece) were some of Paul's most loyal supporters as well as his fellow-sufferers. His kinship with them in their hardship was particularly poignant as he wrote to them from a Roman prison.

What to watch for in Philippians: Notice how many times Paul mentions joy in Philippians, which is remarkable given that both the author and recipients of the letter were experiencing severe persecution.

1 TIMOTHY, TITUS, AND 2 TIMOTHY

Paul's final letters were written to his two young protégés to help them bring order to renegade churches in Ephesus and Crete and appoint properly qualified leaders.

What to watch for in 1 Timothy, Titus and 2 Timothy: Look for a different side to Paul's character than has been evident in other letters. Rather than the fierce leader, we see the affectionate mentor and fatherly friend.

 **PERSONAL BIBLE EXPERIENCE**

Your personal Bible experience starts with a daily practice of reading the Bible. This week before your group meeting, read the last part of Romans and the books of Colossians, Ephesians, Philemon, Philippians, 1 Timothy, Titus, and 2 Timothy. Use the journaling space to capture your thoughts, questions, responses, emotions, and insights as you read the daily selection. Keep in mind the questions you will be talking about with your discussion group:

- What was new or compelling to you?
- What questions did you have?
- Was there anything that bothered you?
- What did you learn about loving God?
- What did you learn about loving others?

Daily Reading Journal

Day 16: Romans 9:1–16:27 (pages 177–188)

_____

_____

_____

_____

_____

_____

Day 17: Colossians Invitation–4:18 (pages 189–195)

_____

_____

_____

_____

_____

_____

Day 18: Ephesians Invitation–Philemon 25 (pages 197–210)

_____

_____

_____

_____

_____

_____

Day 19: Philippians Invitation–1 Timothy 6:21 (pages 211–226)

_____

_____

_____

_____

_____

_____

Day 20: Titus Invitation–2 Timothy 4:22 (pages 227–238)

_____

_____

_____

_____

_____

 **COMMUNITY BIBLE EXPERIENCE**

Welcome to Session 4 of the Community Bible Experience. You have been experiencing the Bible personally by reading the last part of Romans and the books of Colossians, Ephesians, Philemon, Philippians, 1 Timothy, Titus, and 2 Timothy this week, and now your group has gathered to experience the Bible in community with each other. Think of your discussion as more of a book club than a Bible study.

Reflecting on the Previous Week (30–60 minutes)

From your Personal Bible Experience in Romans, Colossians, Ephesians, Philemon, Philippians, 1 Timothy, Titus, and 2 Timothy this week, have a conversation with your group about what you read by answering the following questions.

What was new or compelling to you?

What questions did you have?

Was there anything that bothered you?

What did you learn about loving God?

What did you learn about loving others?

Preparing for the Week Ahead (15–20 minutes)

WATCH VIDEO WEEK 5: MATTHEW

To get the most out of what you will be reading in the coming week, close your time together by watching the video of Bible teacher Jeff Manion explaining the themes and relevance of Matthew. Use the following outline to jot down any additional insights or questions.

VIDEO NOTES

Matthew

Matthew—called from being a tax collector to a follower of Christ

Matthew's banquet for the tax collectors and sinners

> "For the Son of Man came to seek and to save the lost."
>
> (LUKE 19:10)

Relevance of Matthew

It doesn't matter what you have done; Christ calls you to follow him.

Themes of Matthew

Fulfillment of prophecy

Jesus's life replicating the history of Israel—Jesus as founder of a restored Israel

Non-Jewish people coming to Jesus

> Then Jesus came to them and said, "All authority in heaven
> and on earth has been given to me. Therefore go and make
> disciples of all nations, baptizing them in the name of the
> Father and of the Son and of the Holy Spirit, and teaching
> them to obey everything I have commanded you. And sure-
> ly I am with you always, to the very end of the age."
>
> (MATTHEW 28:18–20)

Jesus's authority

Relevance of Matthew

Does Christ have authority over you?

THIS WEEK

· · · · · · · · · ·

Read the book of Matthew in *The Books of the Bible, New Testament.* Maintain your momentum by keeping these guidelines in mind:

- Read what you can.
- Read something every day.
- Always have your *Books of the Bible* with you.
- Every week is a new week.
- Use this study journal as you do your reading for Week 5: Matthew, recording any thoughts on the Daily Reading Journal pages.

MATTHEW

Matthew, the beginning of the second group of books in the New Testament, tells the story of Jesus from a Jewish perspective, presenting him as Israel's promised Messiah. The book does this by drawing a number of parallels between Jesus and Moses, including:

- They both narrowly escaped an attempt on their lives as infants.
- Moses spent 40 years in the wilderness before his ministry; Jesus spent 40 days in the wilderness before his ministry.
- Moses gave people the Torah which was divided into five books. Matthew organizes the teachings of Jesus into five long speeches.
- Moses went up Mount Sinai to receive the law; Jesus gave his first speech on a mountain.
- Moses instituted the Passover; Jesus became the ultimate Passover lamb.

What to watch for in Matthew: Look for the five speeches of Jesus (which each end with "When Jesus had finished saying these things . . ."), and notice how the events leading up to the speech tie in to each of the five themes.

 **PERSONAL BIBLE EXPERIENCE**

Your personal Bible experience starts with a daily practice of reading the Bible. This week before your group meeting, read the book of Matthew. Use the journaling space to capture your thoughts, questions, responses, emotions, and insights as you read the daily selection. Keep in mind the questions you will be talking about with your discussion group:

- What was new or compelling to you?
- What questions did you have?
- Was there anything that bothered you?
- What did you learn about loving God?
- What did you learn about loving others?

Daily Reading Journal

Day 21: Matthew Invitation–7:29 (pages 239–251)

_____

_____

_____

_____

_____

_____

Day 22: Matthew 8:1–13:52 (pages 251–262)

_____

_____

_____

_____

_____

Day 23: Matthew 13:53–18:35 (pages 262–270)

_____

_____

_____

_____

_____

Day 24: Matthew 19:1–25:46 (pages 270–283)

_____

_____

_____

_____

_____

_____

Day 25: Matthew 26:1–28:20 (pages 283–290)

_____

_____

_____

_____

_____

COMMUNITY BIBLE EXPERIENCE

Welcome to Session 5 of the Community Bible Experience. You have been experiencing the Bible personally by reading through the book of Matthew this week, and now your group has gathered to experience the Bible in community with each other. Think of your discussion as more of a book club than a Bible study.

Reflecting on the Previous Week (30–60 minutes)

From your Personal Bible Experience in Matthew this week, have a conversation with your group about what you read by answering the following questions.

What was new or compelling to you?

What questions did you have?

Was there anything that bothered you?

What did you learn about loving God?

What did you learn about loving others?

Preparing for the Week Ahead (15–20 minutes)

WATCH VIDEO WEEK 6: HEBREWS, JAMES, MARK

To get the most out of what you will be reading in the coming week, close your time together by watching the video of Bible teacher Jeff Manion explaining the themes and relevance of Hebrews, James, and Mark. Use the following outline to jot down any additional insights or questions.

VIDEO NOTES

Hebrews

Written to Jewish believers suffering intense persecution

> Sometimes you were publicly exposed to insult and
> persecution; at other times you stood side by side with
> those who were so treated. You suffered along with those
> in prison and joyfully accepted the confiscation of your
> property.
>
> (HEBREWS 10:33–34)

Jewish Christians were tired from persecution and tempted to escape by returning to Judaism.

Purpose of Hebrews

Draws the contrast between the old system and Jesus's new system

To encourage perseverance

Recall heroes of the faith (Hebrews 11)

Relevance of Hebrews

The journey of following God has always been a journey of trust.

James

Topics of James

How faith impacts our daily walk

Using wealth wisely to honor God

Taming the tongue

Faith without works is dead.

Relevance of James

Scripture is intended not for information but transformation.

Ask: How am I allowing the Word of God to transform my life?

Mark

The writer of action

Writing to a Gentile audience in Rome, Mark is intent on
communicating Jesus clearly in different cultural contexts.

Focus of Mark

Mark presents Jesus's authority.

One-third of Mark is spent on Jesus's death.

Jesus's suffering for us can encourage perseverance in
persecution.

Relevance of Hebrews, James, and Mark

Persevere and cling to Christ.

THIS WEEK

Read the books of Hebrews, James, and Mark in *The Books of the Bible,
New Testament*. Maintain your momentum by keeping these guidelines
in mind:

- Read what you can.
- Read something every day.
- Always have your *Books of the Bible* with you.
- Every week is a new week.
- Use this study journal as you do your reading for Week 6:
  Hebrews, James, Mark, recording any thoughts on the Daily
  Reading Journal pages.

HEBREWS, JAMES, MARK

HEBREWS

The writer of Hebrews warns Jewish Christians against hiding their Christian identity behind their Jewish practices to escape persecution. He argues that Jesus offers a salvation more complete and permanent than that of the Law of Moses; Jesus is leading us to a promised land that overshadows that of the Israelites; Jesus is a greater high priest than those serving in the Jewish temple.

What to watch for in Hebrews: With its rich imagery and complex theology, Hebrews is one of the most challenging books in the New Testament. If you find yourself getting bogged down, focus on the call in the last section (pages 319–323) to respond to all God has done for us by stepping out in faith.

JAMES

This book by one of Jesus's brothers was addressed to Jewish believers scattered throughout the Roman Empire, and it focuses on questions of daily living: the pursuit of wisdom, caring for the poor, the responsible use of wealth, controlling the tongue, and more.

What to watch for in James: This book should be read, not like the epistles, which were letters, but like the book of Proverbs, which is a collection of sayings. Slow down and allow time to ponder each nugget of wisdom.

MARK
· · · · · ·

The book of Mark begins the third group of New Testament books: those written or influenced by Peter. Mark was written to a Roman audience, and appears to be the recording of the memoirs of Mark's fellow ministry partner, Peter. Mark highlights the importance of being willing to suffer for Jesus.

What to watch for in Mark: Mark is a master storyteller, and his gospel moves at a breakneck speed. Try reading this book as quickly as you comfortably can, and allow yourself to get caught up in the building tension of this action-packed drama.

 **PERSONAL BIBLE EXPERIENCE**
· ·

Your personal Bible experience starts with a daily practice of reading the Bible. This week before your group meeting, read the books of Hebrews, James, and Mark. Use the journaling space to capture your thoughts, questions, responses, emotions, and insights as you read the daily selection. Keep in mind the questions you will be talking about with your discussion group:

- What was new or compelling to you?
- What questions did you have?
- Was there anything that bothered you?
- What did you learn about loving God?
- What did you learn about loving others?

Daily Reading Journal

Day 26: Hebrews Invitation–4:13 (pages 291–297)

_____

_____

_____

_____

_____

Day 27: Hebrews 4:14–13:25 (pages 297–309)

_____

_____

_____

_____

_____

Day 28: James Invitation–5:20 (pages 311–318)

_____

_____

_____

_____

Day 29: Mark Invitation–8:30 (pages 319–334)

_____

_____

_____

_____

Day 30: Mark 8:31–16:20 (pages 334–350)

_____

_____

_____

_____

_____

 **COMMUNITY BIBLE EXPERIENCE**

Welcome to Session 6 of the Community Bible Experience. You have been experiencing the Bible personally by reading through the books of Hebrews, James, and Mark this week, and now your group has gathered to experience the Bible in community with each other. Think of your discussion as more of a book club than a Bible study.

Reflecting on the Previous Week (30–60 minutes)

From your Personal Bible Experience in Hebrews, James, and Mark this week, have a conversation with your group about what you read by answering the following questions.

What was new or compelling to you?

What questions did you have?

Was there anything that bothered you?

What did you learn about loving God?

What did you learn about loving others?

Preparing for the Week Ahead (15–20 minutes)

WATCH VIDEO WEEK 7: 1–2 PETER, JUDE, JOHN

To get the most out of what you will be reading in the coming week, close your time together by watching the video of Bible teacher Jeff Manion explaining the focus and relevance of 1–2 Peter, Jude, and John. Use the following outline to jot down any additional insights or questions.

VIDEO NOTES

1 Peter

Peter's darkest moment: His betrayal. Then Jesus restores Peter.

Relevance: Jesus is not done with us yet, no matter the failure

Peter writes thirty years after the crucifixion.

Focus of 1 Peter

Our high calling as children of God and a call to live a holy life

Persecution and how to endure it, based on the example of Jesus's manner of suffering

2 Peter and Jude

New crisis: Is Jesus coming back?

Jesus will keep his promise to return and will restore the world.

Relevance of 1–2 Peter and Jude

Live lives that are separated to God.

John

Structure of John

Synoptic Gospels: Matthew, Mark, and Luke

John includes different material and perspective.

Cadence of John: Miracle followed by speech or sermon

John opens with the same words as Genesis: In the beginning . . .

Significance: Jesus brings a brand new creation.

John Uses Signs to Point to Jesus

Feeding of the 5,000 and Jesus as the Bread of Life

Raising of Lazarus and Jesus as the Resurrection and Life

Healing of the blind man and Jesus as the Light of the World

Relevance of John

Believing in who Jesus is . . .

for those who are exploring their faith

for those who question their faith

for those with a worn-out faith

THIS WEEK

Read the books of 1–2 Peter, Jude and John in *The Books of the Bible, New Testament*. Maintain your momentum by keeping these guidelines in mind:

- Read what you can.
- Read something every day.
- Always have your *Books of the Bible* with you.
- Every week is a new week.
- Use this study journal as you do your reading for Week 7: 1–2 Peter, Jude, John, recording any thoughts on the Daily Reading Journal pages.

WEEK 7
1–2 PETER, JUDE, JOHN

1 PETER

Peter wrote letters to encourage believers in what is now Turkey. The main point of his first letter is to encourage believers to remain faithful in the face of intense persecution.

What to watch for in 1 Peter: Think of Peter's own story as you read about suffering for the faith. This is the man who caved under the scrutiny of a servant girl! How far he has come, and how deeply he understands both the irony of his own history and the dichotomy of being able to rejoice as one participates in the sufferings of Christ.

2 PETER AND JUDE

It appears that Peter read a copy of Jude's letter and felt compelled to address the same issue with his readers. Both writers address a dangerous false teaching that contended that because Jesus had not returned already, his return couldn't be expected at all; therefore they could live immoral lives because they didn't expect any future judgment.

What to watch for in 2 Peter and Jude: As you read, think about how you can "contend for the faith" while giving people space to process their doubts and ask honest questions.

JOHN

The book of John marks the fourth and final group of New Testament books. These are written that you may believe that Jesus is the Messiah, the Son of God, and that by believing you may have life in his name. John is hereby making the issue of belief central to his purpose in telling Jesus's story.

What to watch for in John: Notice how the number seven features prominently in John's gospel. For instance, you'll read of seven miracles Jesus performs and seven "I am" statements he proclaims. To the Jewish people, the number seven represented completeness or wholeness—a finished work of God.

 **PERSONAL BIBLE EXPERIENCE**

Your personal Bible experience starts with a daily practice of reading the Bible. This week before your group meeting, read the books of 1–2 Peter, Jude, and John. Use the journaling space to capture your thoughts, questions, responses, emotions, and insights as you read the daily selection. Keep in mind the questions you will be talking about with your discussion group:

- What was new or compelling to you?
- What questions did you have?
- Was there anything that bothered you?
- What did you learn about loving God?
- What did you learn about loving others?

Daily Reading Journal

Day 31: 1 Peter Invitation–5:14 (pages 351–358)

_____

_____

_____

_____

_____

Day 32: 2 Peter Invitation–Jude 25 (pages 359–368)

_____

_____

_____

_____

_____

Day 33: John Invitation–6:71 (pages 369–382)

_____

_____

_____

_____

_____

Day 34: John 7:1–12:50 (pages 382–395)

_____

_____

_____

_____

_____

Day 35: John 13:1–21:25 (pages 395–408)

_____

_____

_____

_____

_____

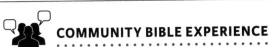 **COMMUNITY BIBLE EXPERIENCE**

Welcome to Session 7 of the Community Bible Experience. You have been experiencing the Bible personally by reading through the books of 1–2 Peter, Jude, and John this week, and now your group has gathered to experience the Bible in community with each other. Think of your discussion as more of a book club than a Bible study.

Reflecting on the Previous Week (30–60 minutes)

From your Personal Bible Experience in 1–2 Peter, Jude, and John this week, have a conversation with your group about what you read by answering the following questions.

What was new or compelling to you?

What questions did you have?

Was there anything that bothered you?

What did you learn about loving God?

What did you learn about loving others?

Preparing for the Week Ahead (15–20 minutes)

WATCH VIDEO WEEK 8: 1–3 JOHN, REVELATION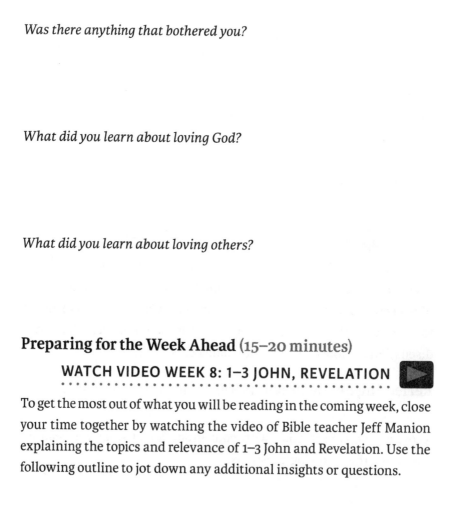

To get the most out of what you will be reading in the coming week, close your time together by watching the video of Bible teacher Jeff Manion explaining the topics and relevance of 1–3 John and Revelation. Use the following outline to jot down any additional insights or questions.

VIDEO NOTES

1 John

Problems Addressed in 1 John

Gnosticism and denial of Jesus's physical body—but we saw Jesus with our own eyes

Belief that sin is of no consequence—but you are called to holiness in your body

Disregard of loving others—let us love one another

2–3 John

How to Deal with Those Causing These Problems

2 John: Warning against false teachers

3 John: Open your homes to the true teachers

Relevance of 1–3 John

Jesus knows what it means to be human.

The importance of love

Revelation

Revelation uses apocalyptic literature, which paints a picture of the seen and unseen world, and the unveiling of the conflict.

Opening Messages from Jesus to Congregations

Affirmation and correction

Jesus's concern for the life and health of the church

Characters in Revelation

The main character is God himself.

Jesus is shown as both the Suffering Servant and Coming King.

Relevance of Revelation

Absorb how the story ends in re-creation.

Bible begins with the presence of God and the loss of his presence, and ends with God's presence returning.

THIS WEEK

Read the books of 1–3 John and Revelation in *The Books of the Bible, New Testament.* Maintain your momentum by keeping these guidelines in mind:

- Read what you can.
- Read something every day.
- Always have your *Books of the Bible* with you.
- Every week is a new week.
- Use this study journal as you do your reading for Week 8: 1–3 John, Revelation, recording any thoughts on the Daily Reading Journal pages.

1–3 JOHN, REVELATION

1 JOHN

John's letters give us a good picture of the church toward the end of the first century AD, which in some cases was a church embroiled in controversy. The one addressed in 1 John is the Greek philosophy that all flesh is evil and only spirit is good. If that was so, how could God have come to earth in a human body? And why do we have to live moral lives?

2–3 JOHN

These letters to different audiences warn churches against providing assistance to false teachers but encourage hospitality toward those promoting the true message of Jesus.

What to watch for in 1–3 John: See if you notice any parallels or similar phrasing between John's letters and John's gospel (for example, *this is how God showed his love among us: He sent his one and only Son into the world that we might live through him*).

REVELATION

John received a vision in which he saw that the cult of emperor worship would soon become deadly to followers of Jesus. He wrote down his vision in a literary form called *apocalypse*, in which a visitor from heaven takes the recipient of the vision on a journey through heaven, using vivid symbols to disclose the secrets of the unseen world and the future. The vision enables the recipients to understand the spiritual dimensions of their situation and to respond to the crisis by remaining loyal to God.

What to watch for in Revelation: Revelation has some of the most puzzling imagery in the Bible. Whatever you make of its content, remember the key message: Stand firm, because in the end, God wins.

 **PERSONAL BIBLE EXPERIENCE**

Your personal Bible experience starts with a daily practice of reading the Bible. This week before your group meeting, read the books of 1–3 John and Revelation. Use the journaling space to capture your thoughts, questions, responses, emotions, and insights as you read the daily selection. Keep in mind the questions you will be talking about with your discussion group:

- What was new or compelling to you?
- What questions did you have?
- Was there anything that bothered you?
- What did you learn about loving God?
- What did you learn about loving others?

Daily Reading Journal

Day 36: 1 John Invitation–3 John 14 (pages 409–423)

_____

_____

_____

_____

_____

Day 37: Revelation Invitation–3:22 (pages 425–431)

_____

_____

_____

_____

Day 38: Revelation 4:1–16:21 (pages 431–444)

_____

_____

_____

_____

_____

_____

Day 39: Revelation 17:1–22:21 (pages 444–453)

_____

_____

_____

_____

_____

Day 40: GRACE DAY

COMMUNITY BIBLE EXPERIENCE

Welcome to Session 8 of the Community Bible Experience. You have been experiencing the Bible personally by reading through the books of 1–3 John and Revelation this week, and now your group has gathered to experience the Bible in community with each other. Think of your discussion as more of a book club than a Bible study.

Reflecting on the Previous Week (30–60 minutes)

From your Personal Bible Experience in 1–3 John and Revelation this week, have a conversation with your group about what you read by answering the following questions.

What was new or compelling to you?

What questions did you have?

Was there anything that bothered you?

What did you learn about loving God?

What did you learn about loving others?

Final Reflections (15–30 minutes)

Reflect: Give each person a chance to share how their journey through the New Testament impacted them, how it shaped their understanding of the Bible, and what implications it might have for their life.

Rejoice: Celebrate your achievement together! Reading through *The Books of the Bible, New Testament* in just eight weeks is a major accomplishment. For some groups, this is the end of your journey through the entire Bible. If you have read all four volumes in *The Books of the Bible* series, rejoice all the more! You have achieved a milestone that for some of you, you may have never thought possible. Take some time to thank each other for providing the community support and encouragement it took to finish this journey together.

Regroup: Plan your next meeting.

For some groups, *The Books of the Bible, New Testament* is your first volume to complete, and now you are moving on to *The Books of the Bible, Covenant History.*

If you are taking a break before you start the next volume of *The Books of the Bible,* choose the date for your introductory session. To whet your appetite for what's next, read the Invitation to the Covenant History on page 15 of this journal.

If you are continuing to *The Books of the Bible, Covenant History* next week, go ahead and watch the video of Bible teacher John Walton explaining the themes and relevance of Genesis, and take notes on pages 18–20 of this journal.

Read and Engage with Scripture in a Whole New Way!

The Books of the Bible is a fresh yet ancient presentation of Scripture ideal for personal or small group use. This 4-part Bible removes chapter and verse numbers, headings, and special formatting so the Bible is easier to read. The Bible text featured is the accurate, readable, and clear New International Version.

To get the entire Bible, look for all four books in *The Books of the Bible*:

Covenant History
Discover the Origins of God's People   9780310448037

The Prophets
Listen to God's Messengers Proclaiming Hope and Truth   9780310448044

The Writings
Find Wisdom in Stories, Poetry, and Songs   9780310448051

New Testament
Enter the Story of Jesus' Church and His Return   9780310448020

The Books of the Bible Study Journal   9780310086055

The Books of the Bible Video Study

9780310086109

Join pastor Jeff Manion and teacher John Walton as they look at the context and purpose for each book of the Bible. Included are (32) 10-minute sessions that can be used with large or small groups.

Kids, Read the Bible in a Whole New Way!

The Books of the Bible is a fresh way for kids to experience Scripture! Perfect for reading together as a family or church group, this 4-part Bible series removes chapter and verse numbers, headings, and special formatting. Now the Bible is easier to read, and reveals the story of God's great love for His people, as one narrative. Features the easy-to-read text of the New International Reader's Version (NIrV). Ages 8-12.

Look for all four books in *The Books of the Bible*:

Covenant History
Discover the Beginnings of God's People   9780310761303

The Prophets
Listen to God's Messengers Tell about Hope and Truth   9780310761358

The Writings
Learn from Stories, Poetry, and Songs   9780310761334

New Testament
Read the Story of Jesus, His Church, and His Return   9780310761310

My Bible Story Coloring Book
The Books of the Bible   9780310761068

The Books of the Bible Children's Curriculum
9780310086161

These engaging lessons are formatted around relatable Scripture references, memory verses, and Bible themes. This curriculum has everything you need for 32 complete lessons for preschool, early elementary, and later elementary classes.